FLORIDA'S BEST
BED & BREAKFASTS
AND
HISTORIC HOTELS

Bruce Hunt

Pineapple Press, Inc.
Sarasota, Florida

For my nieces and nephew:
Cameron, Christine, Taylor, and Ross

Pineapple Press, Inc.
P.O. Box 3889
Sarasota, Florida 34230
www.pineapplepress.com

Library of Congress Cataloging-in-Publication Data

Hunt, Bruce, 1957–
    Florida's best bed & breakfasts and historic hotels / Bruce Hunt. – First
    edition.
            pages cm
Includes index.
ISBN 978-1-56164-605-0 (pbk. : alk. paper)
    1. Bed and breakfast accommodations–Florida–Directories. 2. Historic
hotels–Florida–Directories. 3. Florida–Directories. I. Title. II. Title:
Florida's best bed and breakfasts and historic hotels.

TX907.3.F6H85 2013
917.306'409759–dc23

                    2013011575

First Edition
10 9 8 7 6 5 4 3 2 1

Design by Shé Hicks
Printed in the United States

All photographs are by Bruce Hunt except the back cover photo of Bruce (at Key West Ernest Hemingway Look-alike Contest) by Doug Davidson and the Addison on Amelia House Bed & Breakfast (Fernandina Beach) by Mary Ellen Connelly.

CONTENTS

ACKNOWLEDGMENTS

Thank you to June and David Cussen, Shé Hicks, and Kris Rowland at Pineapple Press. What a privilege and a pleasure it is to work with them. Thanks also to all of the Florida innkeepers who have been most helpful in my research.

INTRODUCTION

Back in the 1960s—my formative years—my brother, sister, and I had a babysitter named Mrs. Spangler, who essentially had become family. She and her husband were retired, and each summer they would load up their camper-top pickup truck and go on the road, always for a month or more at a time. We waited eagerly for the Spanglers' return because Mrs. Spangler always came back with stacks of photographs and amazing stories of the places they had been—Yellowstone National Park, Carlsbad Caverns, the Wild West deserts of Arizona and New Mexico, the Rocky Mountains. Best of all, she always brought back souvenirs for us. I distinctly recall her returning from Petrified Forest National Park in Arizona with chunks of petrified wood. I was mesmerized. They might as well have been chunks of gold. I don't know that I can specifically pinpoint the exact origin of my fascination with travel, but Mrs. Spangler must have had something to do with it.

Perhaps it is appropriate that this book is being released on the 500-year anniversary of Ponce de Leon's arrival in Florida. In a way, Ponce de Leon was Florida's first tourist who came in search of what might be deemed Florida's first tourist attraction, the Fountain of Youth. (Of course he never found it, but he didn't have GPS.) For five hundred years, people have been coming to Florida to discover something new and experience something unfamiliar. As I learned from Mrs. Spangler, that is the very essence of travel.

I spent much of the last twelve months on the road, crisscrossing the state, visiting and photographing bed-and-breakfasts and renovated historic hotels, with an eye out for anything that was new or unfamiliar to me. In this day and age, it may seem like an old-fashioned way to go about my research, but there is simply no substitute for actually visiting each place. No, it's not the most cost-effective way of doing it; it's just the best way. Kind of like the hotel and bed-and-breakfast businesses themselves: It's not the best way to make your fortune. Profit margins, if they exist at all, are thin, the hours are long, and unexpected pitfalls lurk around every corner, particularly in historic structures. Many bed-and-breakfast owners also live at work. Imagine strangers staying in your home seven nights a week! For successful owners, the love of maintaining a historic place and the personal satisfaction from creating a sanctuary for others exceeds their exasperation. It takes a very special type of person to embrace that. Not unexpectedly, some of the lodgings from the last edition have closed. But I was surprised to find that a significant number of the survivors had been remodeled and, in some cases, expanded. I found quite a few new places as well.

Sometimes the lodging itself is the destination. This is certainly the case with historic hotels. More often, the lodging exists because of the locale. In this book, I have spent more time on the background and history of the locations. Advancing age seems to generate greater interest in retrospection. Certainly the older I get, the more drawn I am to a place's past. Not surprisingly, I found the largest number of bed-and-breakfasts and historic hotels in Florida's most historic towns. I found seventeen in St. Augustine, twenty-four in Key West, and eight in Fernandina. So this book is almost as much a discussion of the history of these places and their locations as it is a lodging guidebook.

My first edition of *Florida's Finest Inns and Bed & Breakfasts* came out in 2001, and the second in 2009. In the years since that last edition, much has changed, not just in Florida's lodging offerings but also in how we read books. For the most part, this is the third edition of that book, but so much was new that we decided it deserved a fresh title: *Florida's Best Bed & Breakfasts and Historic Hotels*. It is available as both a printed book and as an e-book. E-book edition readers get some extras: They can link directly to websites, and they can also access an expanded portfolio of photographs right from the book. Readers of the printed book can also access the same photo portfolio by visiting www.brucehuntbooks.com.

In my two decades of travel writing, I have adopted an unconventional research methodology. It is commonplace in the travel-writing industry to give advance notice of your intentions to the owners of a location. Often, they roll out the red carpet. Sometimes they offer to "comp" your stay, or let you stay without charge. I have never accepted a comp. It just rubs against my journalistic ethics. I don't blame the owners. They want to present their business in the most favorable light to get a positive write-up. I, however, want a genuine view of the place and want to experience it just as my readers would. So most of the time, I arrive incognito. When I do find it necessary to interview someone, I usually do so after my visit. One of my most-asked questions at book signings is, "Did you spend the night in all of these places?" The answer, of course, is no. I have stayed in many, about a third of them, some of them multiple times. But I have visited all of them in person with only one exception: Little Palm Island. You can arrive only by boat, you must have a reservation, and, frankly, it is quite expensive. I'll get there one day.

So, what do I mean by "best bed & breakfasts"? I'll confess: My choice of the word "best" had less to do with grading these places and more to do about liking the alliteration. "Appealing" or "intriguing" would probably be a more accurate term. Truth is, all of these places have uniquely appealing attributes. Some are quaint, cozy, or whimsical, like Chalet Suzanne in Lake Wales. Others are grand, historic, and luxurious, like the Breakers in Palm Beach or the Don CeSar on St. Pete Beach. Still others are intimate and luxurious, like the Brazilian Court in Palm Beach. Others are not so much luxurious as they are historically rustic, like the Island Hotel in Cedar Key or the Rod and Gun Club in Everglades City. Some aren't even bed-and-breakfasts or hotels but instead clusters of cottages that I found so charming that I had to include them, like the Bungalow Beach Resort on Bradenton Beach, Castaways on Sanibel, and Cabbage Key Inn. I have always tried to avoid naming favorites (although that doesn't mean I don't have them), but I will say this much: My personal favorites are usually not the most lavish, the most luxurious, or the most opulent. Not that I don't enjoy all of that, but my favorites are usually the rustic, off-the-beaten-path, quirky places.

OK. Start exploring.

A TALE OF TWO HENRYS: FLORIDA'S GRAND HOTELIERS

It's impossible to discuss historic Florida hotels without talking about the two Henrys, Florida's grand hoteliers and railroad magnates: Henry M. Flagler and Henry B. Plant. At the turn of the twentieth century, these two men separately but simultaneously turned Florida's east and west coasts, respectively, from wilderness into civilization.

Henry Flagler's accomplishments in Florida would be impressive if performed today. One hundred years ago, they were positively astonishing. And he did it all at an age when most people have long since retired to a rocking chair on the front porch of Shady Rest. He was a genius, he was a visionary, and he was a philanthropist. Although for much of his life he was driven by an insatiable thirst for prosperity, it seems none of what he achieved in Florida was motivated by profit. It couldn't have been: He lost a fortune. Flagler was a brilliant businessman, but Florida was not about business to him. It was about creativity. The east coast of Florida was Flagler's blank canvas. His railroad tracks through impossible terrain and his castlelike hotels were his art.

Henry Morrison Flagler, a preacher-farmer's son, left his family's farm in Hopewell, New York, when he was only fourteen years old. Even at that age, he understood that he could not be satisfied with the meager life that awaited him if he stayed. He made his way to

Republic, Ohio, to work for his older half-brother, Dan Harkness, at L.G. Harkness and Company, a general store founded by Dan's uncle. Henry was a determined worker, and although his formal education had ended after the eighth grade, he quickly developed sharp business instincts and showed a natural talent for salesmanship. At thirty-two, he invested his life's savings with a partner in a new salt-mining venture. Initially they made money, but at the end of the Civil War, the salt market collapsed, and so did their business. Henry went to work for a grain merchant company called Clark and Sanford in Cleveland. It was here in Cleveland that he and John D. Rockefeller became close friends. At thirty-seven, Henry joined Rockefeller's fledgling firm, which three years later would become the Standard Oil Company.

Flagler married Mary Harkness, one of L.G. Harkness's daughters. In Cleveland, the Flaglers lived on the same street as the Rockefellers and Samuel Andrews, the third partner in their firm. The three worked closely together, but Rockefeller and Flagler were particularly tight.

Petroleum was an emerging product, and new uses were being found for it all the time. In its first two years, Standard Oil tripled its production. Flagler quickly evolved into the firm's contract and negotiations man. He negotiated favorable railroad rates by guaranteeing minimum volumes per day. This gave Rockefeller, Andrews, and Flagler a distinct advantage early in this new industry. Now the smaller competing refineries around Cleveland weren't able to make any money, so Flagler, representing the firm, began buying them out. Naturally, he acquired them at discounted prices.

In January 1870, in order to sell stock and generate more capital, the three partners incorporated under the new name, Standard Oil Company. In later years someone asked John D. Rockefeller if that was his idea, and he responded, "I wish I'd had the brains to think of it. It was Henry M. Flagler." Standard Oil continued to gobble up the little guys, even the tiny ones that were producing only a barrel a day. Within months following its incorporation, the company owned eighty percent of the refining volume in and around Cleveland. They were gaining a reputation for ruthlessness. Many of the complainers, who had little choice but to sell their refineries to Standard Oil, had done so for combinations of cash and stock in Standard Oil. The sellers may have been unhappy at the time, but those who hung on to their Standard Oil stock ultimately became quite wealthy.

The growth of the Standard Oil Company was phenomenal. It spread to the Northeast, acquiring more refineries and forming alliances with others. The three owners used the might of their size to negotiate special rates with railroad and pipeline companies. In 1879 the Standard Oil conglomerate and its associates, together formed as the Standard Alliance, controlled ninety-five percent of the U.S. petroleum industry. Flagler's official title was secretary. His real job was deal-maker.

Now the Standard Oil Alliance had caught the attention of Congress. In 1882 the Alliance became the Standard Oil Trust, the largest business concern in the United States. The public wanted it broken up. The Standard Oil Trust was too big and exercised far too much control over oil, rail, and other related industries. Federal investigations and hearings took place continuously over the following decade. Henry Flagler took the stand and was grilled many times. He said as little as possible but always contended that the Trust's success was no more than the result of hard work and smart business decisions. He and the others fought it as long as they could. Finally, by direction of the United States Supreme Court, the Standard Oil Trust dissolved in 1892. As liquidating trustees, however, the Standard Oil group still maintained what amounted to monopolistic power. It was not until 1911that the group truly dissolved into thirty-five different companies.

The Flaglers moved to New York City in 1877. Mary Flagler's health had been declining for many years. In the winter of 1878, the Flaglers took a trip to Jacksonville, Florida, where Mary's health improved marginally, but sadly, in May 1881, she died. This staggered Henry. He had been a very devoted husband to Mary and father to their two children, Harry and Jennie Louise, but he had also spent a great deal of his life consumed with the business. Now he took a different look at his life. That summer he moved the family to Satansoe, an estate at Mamaroneck on Long Island Sound. From then on, he steadily tapered his involvement in Standard Oil and spent more time with his children. Flagler was still secretary and still owned his stock, but he gradually had less to do with the company's day-to-day operation. Of course, he didn't need to work. By now he was infinitely wealthy.

In June 1883, Henry Flagler remarried. His new wife, Ida Shrouds, had been Mary Flagler's nurse in her last years. Not everyone was as excited about the marriage as Henry. Ida was eighteen years younger than he, reportedly short-tempered, and a compulsive shopper. They delayed their honeymoon until December, when they traveled to Florida, eventually making it to St. Augustine. Henry was enthralled with the town but surprised at the lack of development. They stayed for two months, which was plenty of time for wheels to start turning in Flagler's head.

Two years later, they returned to St. Augustine. A hotel called the San Marco had opened, and there were some other new developments as well. Boston architect Franklin Smith built his Spanish Alhambra–style residence out of a new building material that combined cement and shells, called coquina. St. Augustine was just starting to wake up. Smith mentioned to Flagler his interest in building a hotel. Flagler liked the idea. In March 1885, the city held a celebration honoring Ponce de Leon's landing on Florida's east coast. Perhaps it was the romantic sound of that name, but Henry Flagler's first decision regarding his hotel was that it would be named the Ponce de Leon. He had just become acquainted with a Dr. Andrew Anderson, who owned quite a bit of property in the middle of town, and Flagler bought some of it from him before heading back to New York. When he returned in May, he convinced Dr. Anderson to act as his local representative in the building of the Ponce de Leon Hotel. By December workmen were breaking ground. Flagler liked Franklin Smith's new cement-and-shell building material, a forerunner of concrete, and chose it for the Ponce de Leon. It took more than a thousand workers at a time to mix in the coquina shells, pour the cement, and pack it into the forms. The walls were solid cast and four feet thick.

The 450-room, Spanish Renaissance style Ponce de Leon Hotel was spread across five acres and went way beyond being an architectural marvel. It was (and still is) an enormous and magnificent piece of sculpture. It was designed with fountains, statues, towers, domes, balconies, stained-glass windows, a 700-person, oval-shaped dining hall, and detailed artisans' handwork that no one would even consider incorporating into a hotel project today.

From the start, the process took longer than anticipated. Part of the problem was transporting materials to the site. The narrow-gauge Jacksonville, St. Augustine, and Halifax River Railroad, which ran from Jacksonville to St. Augustine, was woefully inadequate, so Flagler simply bought it and immediately instituted improvements. The fifty-five-year-old, recently retired Standard Oil tycoon had begun the second half of his life with two new avocations: hotelier and railroad baron.

Some of Henry's old Standard Oil pals thought he might have spent too much time in the Florida sun. These were incredibly expensive and risky projects. Flagler was undeterred. He bought the Casa Monica Hotel and renamed it the Cordova Hotel in 1888, a year after Franklin Smith completed it. In 1887 he had begun construction on the Alcazar Hotel, across from the Ponce de Leon and next to the Cordova. The Alcazar, which opened in January 1888, was to be an intimate and less-pricey alternative to the Ponce.

Today the Ponce de Leon Hotel is the main structure on the campus of Flagler College, and the Alcazar contains the Lightner Museum. The Cordova Hotel had been an office building for years. In 1999 it was remodeled and resurrected once again as the Casa Monica Hotel. (Read about it in the St. Augustine chapter.)

In March 1889, Flagler's daughter, Jennie Louise, and her baby died following complications from childbirth. As a monument to her, Flagler built the Venetian Renaissance Memorial Presbyterian Church one block from the Ponce de Leon Hotel. Today both she and Henry Flagler are buried in the mausoleum there. Flagler's other philanthropic pursuits in St. Augustine were many. They included rebuilding the Catholic Church after an 1890 fire and building a hospital in 1889. He was also the major contributor to building City Hall and an African-American school.

Flagler continued to acquire railroads. By the end of 1889, he had purchased an assortment of small rail lines, connecting and improving them. In many instances, he added bridges where ferries had done the job before. His railroad now extended as far south as Daytona. Along the way, he bought a small hotel in Ormond Beach. For a while, he thought that this was as far as he would go. South of Daytona, the coast was mostly wild swampland with just a few small settlements. Plus, there were no existing rail lines to buy. He did, however, own some steamers that ran up and down the Indian River, and they were doing fairly well transporting citrus.

Flagler was not one to remain idle for long, and soon he got the itch to expand south. In 1892 he received his state charter to build railroads as far south as Miami, although he claimed he had no intention of going that far. This would be a more formidable undertaking. Up until now, he had acquired and improved existing rails. Now he would be building a railroad from scratch, much of it through uncharted wilderness.

Construction started in June 1892. By November workers had reached New Smyrna. The next leg, to Lake Worth and what would later become West Palm Beach was more difficult. Swampland had to be filled in before tracks could be laid. It took a year and a half to get there. A month before the railroad arrived, Flagler had already completed his largest hotel yet in record time. Constructed of wood on the east bank of Lake Worth, the Royal Poinciana had 540 rooms. At the time it was completed in February 1892, it was the largest wooden hotel in the world. Two years later, he opened a second hotel on the beach a half mile east. This one, smaller and simpler, was called the Palm Beach Inn. Patrons began referring to it as the Breakers since it was down on the beach where the waves were breaking (Read about it in the Palm Beach chapter.)

The Palm Beach Inn turned into precisely the kind of resort for the wealthy that Henry had envisioned. It was a crowning achievement. Once again, he did not anticipate going any further south, but a lady with an orange grove on the Miami River changed all that.

In 1893 widow Julia Tuttle, who owned considerable acreage in what is now downtown Miami, offered to split her property with Flagler if he would bring his railroad all the way down to Miami. Flagler passed on the offer. Two years later, a devastating February freeze wiped out nearly all of central and north Florida's citrus. Julia Tuttle seized the moment and sent Flagler a cutting of fresh, healthy orange blossoms from her groves, along with a reminder that her offer still stood. Oranges were probably the biggest commodity being shipped north on Flagler's railcars, and Mrs. Tuttle's message hit home this time.

Flagler's railroad arrived in Miami in 1896, and he wasted no time constructing the palatial Royal Palm Hotel, a smaller version of his Royal Poinciana. In the summer of 1899, Miami suffered a deadly outbreak of yellow fever. The city underwent quarantine in October, which added economic disaster to a town already devastated by the epidemic. During the five-month quarantine, Flagler hired those who were healthy but confined and out of work. They built sidewalks, roads, and whatever else they could find that needed improvement. As long as they could find something to work on, Flagler sent them money. No one went hungry, and the town of Miami benefited.

Henry Flagler was a much-loved man, not only for the boom that he almost single-handedly brought on, but also because it was apparent that he genuinely cared about the people in the communities that he developed. Public opinion of him was about to turn, however.

Two years before Henry began developing Miami, he started noticing some odd behavior in his wife, Ida. At first he didn't discuss it with anyone. Then the Flaglers' New York family physician, Dr. George Shelton, told Flagler about a bizarre and delusional conversation he had had with Ida. She told Dr. Shelton that she had magic stones that could cure a barren woman. This occurred not long after she learned that she was unable to bear children. Her mental state continued to deteriorate. Henry was distraught and felt powerless to help her. Her delusions became more pronounced and more frequent. She became convinced that she was in love with the Czar of Russia and that he was in love with her, even though they had never met or communicated. She proclaimed she was destined to marry the czar as soon as Henry died, which she predicted would be soon. This news came to her via her Ouija board. She would experience sudden fits of rage without warning. At one point, she locked herself in her room, claiming that spies had infiltrated the house and were after her. Ida had been under Dr. Shelton's close observation for nearly a year when he finally suggested that it would be best for her to be committed to Choate's Sanitarium in Pleasantville, New York.

After eight months, the doctors at Choate's thought Ida had improved enough to go home. Having her back thrilled Henry, and he went to great lengths to entertain her at their Mamaroneck home. She seemed fine for about a month, and then she relapsed into her previous state of insanity, once again obsessed with the Ouija board and convinced of her impending union with the Czar of Russia. Her doctors became concerned that she might actually try to kill Henry in an attempt to fulfill her delusion. Henry hired many specialists to help her. They recommended that she return to the sanitarium, but Henry didn't want to send her back there. When she became dramatically worse, he hired Dr. Du Jardins and four nurses to care for her full time at their home. At the doctor's recommendation, Flagler moved into a Manhattan hotel and was advised not to see her. Ida's condition worsened. Her violent tantrums grew more frequent. She now lived in a fantasy world where her husband was dead and the Czar of Russia was going to take her away. In March 1897, she was recommitted to the Pleasantville sanitarium. Though he sent flowers to her every week for years, Henry never saw her again.

Two years later, in 1899, Flagler moved his residency from New York to Palm Beach, Florida. Some speculated that it was because divorce was easier to obtain in Florida. At that time, even in Florida, insanity was not a valid reason for divorce. In April 1901, however, a bill designed to change divorce laws went before the Florida State Senate and the House, making incurable insanity grounds for divorce. It passed easily, and Governor Jennings signed it. Immediately newspapers labeled the bill the "Flagler Divorce Law." Few doubted that Henry Flagler had wielded his influence to have the law changed. He didn't do much to hide the fact either. Two months later, he filed for divorce from Ida and the state took two months to grant it. One week after that, Flagler announced his engagement to North Carolinian Mary Lily Kenan. The news was made even more sensational because Mary Kenan was less than half Henry Flagler's age. Most were highly critical of Flagler, but his close friends stuck by him.

In Flagler's defense, he set up a trust run by a trustee for Ida worth more than $2 million. It comprised cash, Standard Oil stock, and property. Her annual income, beyond the expenses of keeping her at the sanitarium, was roughly $100,000 per year. Ida, who had by now completely disconnected from reality, knew none of this. Her trustee eventually moved her to a private cottage on the grounds of another sanitarium, where she lived the remainder of her life.

Another tumultuous chapter in his life had passed, and an aging Henry and his young bride were living full-time in Palm Beach. Aging or not, Henry Flagler had one more monumental task to perform, and this one would be his most audacious.

Even before Flagler's railroad had reached Miami, there was speculation that he might attempt to build an extension all the way down to Key West. The idea captivated him, but he was not going to rush into it. Building a 150-mile railroad that would skip across tiny coral islands but would mostly be elevated over water was something that had never been done. It was something that many claimed couldn't be done. When the green light was given to dig the Panama Canal, Flagler knew the time was right to build his overseas railroad. Key West would be the nearest rail terminal to the canal by three hundred miles.

In 1904 he extended his rail line from Miami down to what is now Homestead. Flagler and his engineers discussed at length where to go from there. One option was to jump from Cape Sable, in the lower Everglades, straight down to Key West, but the final choice was to follow the Keys. Construction began on Flagler's "impossible folly" in the summer of 1905. His engineers predicted it would take three years to reach Key West. It took seven. A workforce of three thousand men labored almost nonstop. It was a logistical nightmare. Railcars brought huge tanks of fresh drinking water in daily. Much of the equipment to drive pilings and pour concrete at sea had to be fabricated just for this job. In October 1906, the concrete bridge trestles were put to the test during a violent hurricane. The trestles survived winds that topped 120 miles per hour, but 70 men in camps built on barges died. In 1909 another huge hurricane struck, but this time, with the men now housed in sturdier lodgings, all survived. The engineers were convinced that the bridge trestles were hurricane-proof but not the train sitting on top of them. So they devised an electric switch that automatically stopped a train before it crossed a bridge if wind sensors detected velocity of fifty miles per hour or greater.

Finally, on January 22, 1912, the first official train arrived in Key West with eighty-two-year-old Henry M. Flagler aboard. The arrival was a grand affair, attended by U. S. politicians, representatives from Cuba, and many Central and South American countries, as well as the entire population of Key West. More trains followed throughout the day. One had come straight through all the way from New York. Florida Governor Gilchrist arrived on the last train. Key West celebrated for days. Henry Flagler had accomplished what nearly everyone had declared impossible.

Fifteen months later, on May 20, 1913, Henry Morrison Flagler died quietly at his home in Palm Beach. No specific cause of death was listed. Newspapers reported that he had died simply of sheer exhaustion.

While Henry Flagler was taming Florida's east coast, Henry Plant was doing the same on the west coast.

Henry Bradley Plant learned about overcoming adversity at a very young age. He was six when his father, his sister, and his aunt all died of typhus. Plant also contracted the disease but managed to survive. When he was eighteen, Plant went to work for the New Haven Steamboat Company in Connecticut as a deck hand on steamers that made the run to New York City and back. In 1842 he married Ellen Blackstone. They had a son named Morton Freeman Plant, and Henry changed jobs so he wouldn't be away from his family. He went to work for the Adams Express Company, an express delivery business. It was there where he developed his business acumen. Hard work and natural talent landed Henry numerous promotions. In 1854, when Adams bought out a delivery company in Georgia in order to expand, they put Henry in charge and moved the Plant family to Augusta.

The Southern division of Adams Express did well under Plant's direction. They delivered everything from currency for the United States Mint to newspapers, and they established connections with every steamship port and railway terminal in the South.

In April 1861, just four days before the first shots of the Civil War were fired at Fort Sumter, Plant met with executives from Adams and offered to buy out the Southern division. War was imminent, and Adams executives knew they wouldn't be able to keep it anyway, so they accepted Plant's offer of $500,000 in notes. Henry named his new company Southern Express. Because of Henry's relationship with Adams, Southern Express was the only major delivery company in the South that was able to transport packages to the North. Sometimes the company even handled North-South prisoner exchanges.

Henry would soon be faced with adversity, however. As Union troops moved down into the Southern states, they took away Southern Express's connections one by one. Then Ellen Plant died of tuberculosis. Doubly devastated, Henry took a sabbatical. When the war finally ended, he began to put the pieces of his company back together. Adams Express had picked up most of his connections taken over during the war and returned them to Southern Express. After all, Adams's executives were still holding Henry Plant's note.

Southern Express had always made its deliveries to railroad terminals. From those points, the railroad companies carried the packages on to their destinations. One of Plant's competitors thought he would try some vertical integration and buy a railroad, the Mobile and Ohio. When he failed to make a go of it, Plant stepped in and bought the railroad from his competitor at a bargain-basement price.

Henry Plant was now in the railroad business—and he was good at it. Southern Express prospered and did particularly well transporting produce, citrus, fish, meat, and other perishables from South to North. Before long, he paid off his Adams note, and his focus shifted to railroads.

Plant's genius was in acquisitions. He recognized potential in an existing operation that was usually in poor financial shape, purchased it for a considerable discount, and then built it into a profitable venture. He acquired the bankrupt Charleston and Savannah Railroad, the Florida Southern Railroad, and the Atlantic and Gulf Railway, which he bought at public auction. Next he diversified into steamships and connected them to his rail terminals. Plant's interconnected transportation system was opening up Florida's citrus, vegetable, and lumber markets to the rest of the country.

Henry Plant had long dreamed of providing a regular transport link between Florida and the West Indies, especially Cuba. He had been to Cuba and saw great promise there in transporting goods and people. Tampa Bay and Charlotte Harbor were his two favorite choices for ports. He arrived in Tampa first.

In order to run tracks between Kissimmee and Tampa, in 1883 Plant purchased the land grants and rights-of-way the State of Florida had granted to the Jacksonville, Tampa, and Key West Railroad, which ran out of money before the land grants could be used. The only problem was that their charter ran out in seven months. Plant got the seventy-five miles of track laid in just over six months.

At first, because Tampa Bay was so shallow, steamers had to anchor out in the bay, and smaller launches would unload freight and passengers. Construction began on Port Tampa in 1888. Plant built docks and ran rails to them. He dredged channels and basins and spent more than $3 million on the project. Phosphate was discovered halfway up the Peace River in 1885, and by 1892, it was Tampa's largest export commodity. Port Tampa was booming.

In 1890 Plant completed his first hotel, the forty-room Port Tampa Inn. One year earlier, a smaller, seven-room annex to the hotel was completed and opened. It was three stories tall and built out over the water on pilings halfway out to the end of the dock. Before it opened, construction had already begun on one of Plant's most beautiful projects: the Tampa Bay Hotel. In the meantime, he also bought the existing 150-room Seminole Hotel in Winter Park.

Henry Plant agreed to build the Tampa Bay Hotel along the banks of the Hillsborough River if the city agreed to construct a bridge over the river to give easy access to the Hillsborough County courthouse on the opposite side. The city built the bridge and also offered property tax incentives. Plant hired architect John A. Wood, who had designed hotels in New York and Georgia. This one would be an exotic, four-story brick structure topped with six towering, Moorish minarets. The elegant interior had horseshoe-arched throughways and windows and a wide, winding mahogany staircase in the lobby. A two-story veranda, with elaborate laced brackets in its roof supports, surrounded the exterior. The Tampa Bay Hotel, which opened on February 5, 1891, featured a dining hall, a café, a drug and sundries shop, a barber shop, and even a billiards room. Guests never needed to leave the premises.

Plant insisted that his hotel rivaled Henry Flagler's Ponce De Leon Hotel in St. Augustine, which had opened in 1888. The Tampa Bay Hotel did fairly well in its first years but never really met Plant's expectations as a resort for the ultra-wealthy. Flagler had beaten him to the punch.

Perhaps the Tampa Bay Hotel reached its peak in 1898 during the Spanish-American War, when troops (including Teddy Roosevelt and his Rough Riders) amassed in Tampa for embarkation to Cuba. It remained a hotel until 1930. In 1933 it became the University of Tampa, which it still is today. During the 1890s, Plant acquired or built six more hotels in Ocala, Kissimmee, Punta Gorda, Fort Myers, Palm Harbor, and Clearwater.

Henry Plant died on June 23, 1899, at the age of eighty. At the time, his various companies employed thirteen thousand people in railroad lines, steamship lines, real estate companies, and hotels.

I find the similarity between these two men's lives remarkable. They both had drive and ambition, rose up from meager backgrounds, took risks, and suffered losses. Ultimately, both were enormously influential in the development of Florida, perhaps more so than anyone else in the state's history. The two men were acquainted with each other. Along the way, some minor business transacted between them or at least between their respective companies. Mostly, however, they were congenial rivals. Though it's never been proven, some speculate that Flagler and Plant had a gentlemen's agreement never to invade each other's coast.

NORTHWEST

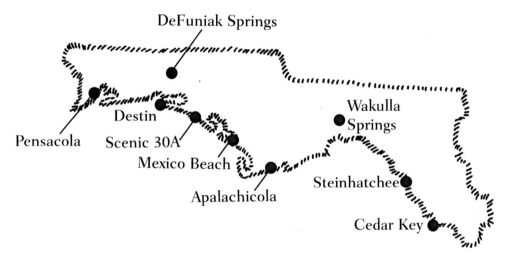

DeFuniak Springs

Pensacola

Destin

Scenic 30A

Mexico Beach

Apalachicola

Wakulla
Springs

Steinhatchee

Cedar Key

PENSACOLA

Florida's westernmost city, Pensacola, is best known for its Naval Air Station, where the Blue Angels are headquartered, and for its glistening white beaches just across the bridge on Pensacola Beach. Visitors might also want to spend some time in Pensacola's Seville Historic District, just east of downtown on Pensacola Bay. Pensacolans are quick to point out that the founding of their city predates St. Augustine by six years. Spanish explorer Don Tristan de Luna built a settlement called Polonza here in 1559. Two years later, it was abandoned after a violent storm sank his fleet. More than a century would pass before Spain returned and built a permanent settlement. Today this quiet and picturesque brick-street neighborhood is home to Historic Pensacola Village with its complex of museums, beautifully restored nineteenth-century cottages, and an assortment of elegant bed-and-breakfasts.

Lee House Bed & Breakfast
400 Bayfront Parkway
Pensacola 32502
(850) 912-8770
www.leehousepensacola.com

The Lee House is actually a new structure, but owners Patrick and Norma Murray made sure that it blended perfectly with the historic neighborhood and matched the architecture of the original 1866 home that once stood on the grounds. Lee House sits on the meandering Bayfront Parkway and overlooks Pensacola Bay. It's also next door to Seville Square, the district's shady-oak park that is a venue for concerts and other festival events. Most of the Lee House's eight spacious suites are decorated to reflect local history or natural scenery, although suite

LEE HOUSE BED & BREAKFAST

seven is contemporary. Six of the suites have French doors leading onto a balcony with views across Pensacola Bay. Suite eight is a corner room with a particularly nice panoramic view.

Noble Manor Bed & Breakfast
110 West Strong Street
Pensacola 32501
(850) 434-9544
(877) 598-4634
www.noblemanor.com

Noble Manor is a circa-1905, Victorian Tudor–style home in the Noble Hill section of Pensacola's historic district. The venue has five rooms, four in the main house and a suite in the adjacent carriage house, as well as a pool and hot tub.

NOBLE MANOR BED & BREAKFAST

RUSSELL ROOST BED & BREAKFAST

Russell Roost Bed & Breakfast
205 Cevallos Street
Pensacola 32502
(850) 429-1231
www.russellroostbedandbreakfast.com

Russell Roost Bed & Breakfast is tucked away in a residential neighborhood in Pensacola's historic district. It was built in 1997 and reminds me of a Mississippi river boat, with two-story verandas that wrap around two sides. The entire facility was designed for ease of handicap access, with ramps and wide doors. Russell Roost has just three rooms, each with French doors that open onto the verandas. All of the rooms are equipped with handicap-accessible bathrooms, and one room has a Jacuzzi tub. The owners will even pick you up at the airport.

DESTIN

Henderson Park Inn Bed & Breakfast
2700 Scenic Highway 98
Destin 32541
(866) 398-4432
www.hendersonparkinn.com

This picturesque beachfront inn could fit in perfectly on Block Island, Rhode Island, or Nantucket, Massachusetts, with its shingle shake siding, steep green roof, and wide curving veranda. It's actually two buildings, both of which have three stories. There are twenty suites in one and fifteen in the other. All are roomy and well appointed: Most have Jacuzzis, refrigerators, and microwaves. The largest, the Presidential Suite, has two bathrooms and two balconies, one off the living room and one off the bedroom. Each suite is furnished with reproduction Victorian furniture and has a private balcony or porch that overlooks the Gulf of Mexico as well as one of the most beautiful beaches in Florida. The Henderson Park Inn's property borders the Henderson Beach State Park so guests can take a long stroll on an undeveloped beach.

Brothers Bill and Steve Abbot, who had previously managed bed-and-breakfasts in Maine, built the inn in 1992. In September 2004, Hurricane Ivan slammed the Panhandle's coastline and caused enough damage to the inn that it had to close. In 2005 Dunavant Enterprises out of Memphis, Tennessee, bought the inn and spent the next year and a half rebuilding it. Henderson Park Inn reopened in May 2007 with even more amenities and a new restaurant called Beach Walk Café, which has earned a reputation as one of the best restaurants in Destin and the only fine-dining restaurant right on the beach.

HENDERSON PARK INN BED & BREAKFAST

Scenic 30A, Walton County

Walton County Road 30A, often referred to as Scenic 30A, dips down off of Highway 98, halfway between Destin and Panama City Beach, to wind along the coast for nineteen miles. Before the 1980s, it was simply an off-the-beaten-path route to Grayton Beach State Park and to the small beachfront communities of Seagrove and Grayton Beach, nestled among the sand dunes and scrub oaks. It has always been scenic. Road 30A's beaches consistently rank among the top five most beautiful in the United States. Their blinding white sand consists of powdered quartz washed down over the eons from the Appalachian Mountains. It squeaks when you walk on it.

About halfway down 30A, on eighty acres of undeveloped land inherited from his grandfather, developer Robert Davis built the town of Seaside next to Seagrove, where Davis had spent every summer as a child. In 1981 he and his wife, Daryl, built a one-story, wood-frame beach cottage with a tin roof. It set the tone for what would become the much-heralded model for New Urbanism. Inspired by the memories of those childhood summers, Davis envisioned a small beach town with shell pathways winding between wood-frame bungalows. He enlisted architects Andres Duany and Elizabeth Plater-Zyberk at Arquitectonica in Miami to help plan the layout and draw up the town's building code. They wanted a town design that would maximize the interaction among neighbors and have its living quarters within easy walking distance of its commercial center. In short, they wanted a pre-sprawl, small suburban town.

It caught on in a much bigger way than anyone imagined. While its planners originally envisioned a town with mostly year-round residents, Seaside proved most popular as a resort destination. Some of Seaside's residents do live there year-round, but for most, this is their second home, and the majority of the cottages can be rented through the Seaside Cottage Rental Agency.

Even before the popular 1998 Jim Carrey movie *The Truman Show* brought national attention to Seaside, other developers had begun to jump on the 30A bandwagon. In 1995, ten miles down the road at the east end of 30A, the first homes went up at Rosemary Beach. Once again, architects Duany and Plater-Zyberk were hired to plan the 107-acre town. Like Seaside, it would be small and pedestrian focused with a commercial center and a Main Street that crossed 30A. They didn't want a Seaside copy, though. Rosemary Beach would have more of a small, coastal European village feel. They looked at the old colonial architecture of the West Indies for inspiration, as well as New Orleans' French Quarter and Old Town St. Augustine. Steep roofs, tall windows, second-floor overhanging balconies, and small courtyards are consistent features here.

Meanwhile, St. Joe Company—an outgrowth of Edward Ball's St. Joe Paper (see Wakulla Lodge chapter) and the largest landowner in northwest Florida—began building Watercolor on five hundred acres that bordered and wrapped around behind Seaside. Watercolor stuck to Seaside's architectural style, but it was on a piece of property too large to walk from one side to the other.

When Seaside first went up, traffic increased somewhat on the winding, two-lane 30A. Traffic increased a bit more as Rosemary Beach developed, although much of its traffic funneled on and off of nearby Highway 98 instead of onto Scenic Highway 30A. As Watercolor developed, traffic increased dramatically, particularly in the high-season months. Although all of these developments have gone to great lengths to maintain the local ecology and the original communities of Grayton Beach and Seagrove are still there, there can be no doubt that 30A's off-the-beaten-path character has been altered.

HIBISCUS COFFEE & GUEST HOUSE BED & BREAKFAST

Hibiscus Coffee & Guest House Bed & Breakfast
85 DeFuniak Street
Grayton Beach 32459
(850) 231-2733
www.hibiscusflorida.com

The little community of Grayton Beach, next door to beautiful Grayton Beach State Park, proudly hangs on to its "Redneck Riviera" roots. Established in the 1890s, it is a 30A original. Seaside's architects got much of their house design inspiration from Grayton Beach cottages, some dating back to the 1920s and '30s.

Hibiscus Guest House is a cluster of pine tree–shaded, two-story houses with thirteen rooms and its own coffee shop, Hibiscus Café. I stayed in the Art Deco room, which has a few odd decorations, like a 1950s' free-standing salon hair dryer. The room also has a screened front porch, which it shares with the coffee shop, and a door that leads to the backyard garden, where the owners sometimes host small concerts and weddings. For breakfast, guests can choose pancakes, waffles, French toast, or frittatas, all served in the café, which is also open for lunch.

Pensione Inn
78 Main Street
Rosemary Beach 32461
(866) 348-8952
www.rosemarybeach.com

Rosemary Beach is designed to feel very much like a coastal Italian village, and the Pensione Inn fits that impression perfectly. The four-

PENSIONE INN

story, red-stucco boutique inn (nine rooms and two suites) was designed by Miami architectural firm Trelles Cabarrocas and completed in 2001. In 2012 it underwent a major interior remodel. The inn anchors the south end of Rosemary Beach's quaint Main Street across from its Western Green park and a boardwalk that crosses the steep dunes onto the beach. In keeping with the European style, my room was small but luxuriously furnished. The larger of the two suites, at six hundred square feet, adds a kitchen and a sitting area with a sleeper sofa. Onano, a tiny Italian café, occupies the inn's first floor.

SEASIDE COTTAGE RENTAL AGENCY

Seaside Cottage Rental Agency
Seaside 32459
(866) 966-2565
www.cottagerentalagency.com

For a number of years, Seaside had only one bed-and-breakfast. In its last iteration, it was called Seaside Avenue Bed & Breakfast, but it sold in 2012 and is now a private residence. With more than two hundred cottage and house rentals, plus nine vintage-style motor court motel rooms, Seaside Cottage Rentals can handle a wide array of accommodations. The pastel-painted cottages range from tiny, one-bedroom getaways up to five-bedroom family compounds, but no two are exactly alike. The motor court resembles a classic 1950s' roadside drive-up motel, like something you might have found on Route 66.

Watercolor Inn
34 Goldenrod Circle
Santa Rosa Beach 32459
(866) 426-2656
www.watercolorresort.com

The four-story Watercolor Inn features sixty comfortably appointed, spacious beachfront rooms ranging from five hundred to six hundred feet in size. The inn also houses the Fish Out of Water restaurant. The Watercolor Resort Inn & Resort Agency handles reservations for Watercolor's cottages, villas, and townhouses as well as the inn.

DeFuniak Springs

DeFuniak Springs was chosen as Florida's Chautauqua winter assembly location in 1884. The Chautauqua Association, based in Lake Chautauqua, New York, promoted a combination of adult education, recreation, and religion. Subsequently, the Florida Chautauqua Association became a defining force for DeFuniak Springs, significantly influencing education and society.

DeFuniak Springs has a considerable collection of historic buildings and homes. Many, like the 1886 Walton-DeFuniak Library, are on Circle Drive, which surrounds Lake DeFuniak. On Baldwin Avenue, DeFuniak Springs' main street, renovated brick storefronts overlook the lake and the restored L&N train depot, now home to the Walton County Heritage Museum.

My favorite downtown lunch spot, the Busy Bee, located a block off Baldwin on Seventh, has been there since 1916.

Hotel DeFuniak
400 East Nelson Avenue
DeFuniak Springs 32433
(850) 892-4383
www.hoteldefuniak.com

This charming two-story, eleven-room hotel was originally built as a Masonic lodge in 1920. The Masons held meetings upstairs and rented the downstairs to a furniture store. Following the collapse of the Florida real estate boom, in 1929 the building sold at a foreclosure auction to attorney Stealie Preacher, who opened his law office downstairs. Preacher's wife turned the upstairs into the Lake Hotel. In the 1940s, it sold again to pharmacist Marshall Lightfoot, who kept the hotel upstairs and opened a drugstore downstairs. Like so many downtown historic structures everywhere, the building had fallen into disrepair by the 1970s. It wasn't until 1996 that a local group purchased it, spent a year restoring it, and then reopened it as the Hotel DeFuniak. Tom and Pam Hutchens had recently moved to DeFuniak Springs and restored a house. In 2003 they decided to buy the hotel. The Hutchens have done a marvelous job of decorating with period antiques to create a genuine 1920s' ambience.

HOTEL DEFUNIAK

MEXICO BEACH

Driftwood Inn
2105 Highway 98
Mexico Beach 32410
(850) 648-5126
www.driftwoodinn.com

It's the best free show on the beach: Pull up an Adirondack chair and watch F-22 Raptor fighter jets from Tyndall Air Force Base (just west of Mexico Beach) perform mock dogfights over the Gulf. The best place to find that Adirondack chair is at the Driftwood Inn, a Mexico Beach icon since the early 1950s. It had been through some alterations by the time Tom and Peggy Wood bought it in 1975. After a fire destroyed the main building in 1994, the Woods decided to rebuild in a Victorian architectural style that mirrored the original tin roof, stick-frame beach house. In the years since, they have added cottages, boardwalks, and a playground. Eventually the Driftwood became its own self-contained beachside village, more rustic than refined. There's even a tiny beachside wedding chapel. Don't be startled by the Driftwood's official greeter, an enormous black-and-white Great Dane named Woody. He's a sweetheart.

DRIFTWOOD INN

APALACHICOLA

It may be in the middle of the Florida Panhandle's "Forgotten Coast," but there is nothing forgettable about Apalachicola's great seafood or its picturesque location at the mouth of the Apalachicola River. Known as the Oyster Capital (ninety percent of Florida's oysters come from here), Apalachicola has worked hard to maintain its status as a working town whose livelihood has been tied to the sea for centuries. And in recent decades, residents have worked equally hard to preserve the town's history and historic structures, making Apalachicola a magnet for visitors.

Sometimes visitors fall in love with Apalachicola and decide to stay. That was the case for Michael Koun, who arrived in 1983 and bought a dilapidated downtown, three-story Victorian hotel called the Gibson Inn. Koun's restoration helped kick off a wave of renovation that spread throughout downtown and into the neighboring residential area.

The Apalachicola River has always been the town's lifeblood. In the 1820s, Apalachicola was a big cotton shipping port. From the 1860s to 1880s, sponge harvesting was big until the industry moved to Tarpon Springs. In the late 1880s, cypress, oak, and pine milling and shipping revitalized the town. Then, in the 1920s, it became the center of Florida's booming seafood industry. Visitors notice right away that the downtown streets are unusually wide. They were built back in the cotton-shipping days so that cotton, unloaded from barges at the docks, could be stacked on the streets and compressed before being moved into the warehouses. Those wide streets make it easy to park anywhere and walk the entire downtown.

Superb restaurants abound in Apalachicola and it's no surprise that seafood is prominent on every menu. Three of my favorites are the Owl Café (a block from the waterfront on Avenue D), Tamara's Café on Market Street, and Up the Creek Raw Bar, which overlooks the river at the end of Water Street.

Consulate Suites
76 Water Street
Apalachicola 32320
(850) 653-1515
(877) 239-1159
www.consulatesuites.com

The red-brick J.E. Grady and Company Building at 76 Water Street was built in 1900 to replace a wooden 1884 building destroyed by a waterfront fire earlier that year. John Grady operated his ship chandlery business downstairs and rented upstairs office space to the French consulate. In 1998, following a three-year renovation, the Grady Market, a clothing, art, and antiques store, opened downstairs, and the Consulate Suites opened upstairs. I stayed for a weekend in the thirteen-hundred-square-foot Consul Room. It has two bedrooms,

CONSULATE SUITES

two baths, a full kitchen, and a sweeping balcony that overlooks the shrimp and oyster boats docked on the riverfront. Its eleven-foot-high stamped-tin ceilings, wide-plank pine floors, and comfortable furnishings made me feel very much at home.

Coombs House Inn
80 Sixth Street
Apalachicola 32320
(850) 653-9199
(888) 244-8320
www.coombshouseinn.com

Some of the palatial homes in the neighborhood on the west side of

COOMBS HOUSE INN

downtown belonged to wealthy turn-of-the-century lumber barons. The Coombs House, built in 1905 by Apalachicola lumber baron James Coombs, is now an elegant bed-and-breakfast. Much of the interior was constructed from the hearty black cypress from which Coombs made his fortune, including the paneled walls in the foyer, the floors, the massive ceiling trusses, and, most notably, the grand staircase. Interior decorator Lynn Wilson, known for her renovation work on historic hotels like the Biltmore in Coral Gables and the Vinoy in St. Petersburg, bought the Coombs House from the Coombs family in 1992. She and her husband, Bill, spent several years rebuilding and restoring it, turning it into a Victorian showcase. In 1998 Lynn and Bill bought and restored the 1911 Dr. Marks House, one block east, and added Camillia Hall, a separate reception room with a large garden yard and a gazebo for weddings and other special events.

Gibson Inn
51 Avenue C
Apalachicola 32320
(850) 653-2191
www.gibsoninn.com

The 1907 Gibson Inn is the centerpiece of Apalachicola's Historic District. When the National Trust for Historic Preservation published its coffee-table book, *America Restored* (Preservation Press), the Gibson Inn was one of the two Florida buildings featured. The three-story Victorian hotel, with verandas wrapping around three of its sides and a cupola-capped tin roof, is the first thing you see after crossing the Highway 98 bridge over the Apalachicola River.

It was the Franklin Inn when James Fulton Buck opened it in 1907. The name changed when sisters Annie and Mary Ellen Gibson bought it in 1923. These were grand years at the inn, but the opulence of that era declined with the passing decades. The Gibson Inn had been boarded up for some time when in 1983, Michael Koun, his brother Neal, and some investor friends bought the hotel for $90,000. Over the next two years, they spent more than $1 million meticulously rebuilding and restoring it to its turn-of-the-century grandeur. Their

GIBSON INN

best architectural reference was a collection of old photos taken in 1910. The photographer had spent that year photographing Apalachicola and the surrounding area. A number of his pictures hang on the walls in the Gibson Inn's dining room.

Four-poster beds and other period antiques decorate each of the Gibson Inn's thirty-one guest rooms. Wooden slat blinds shade the windows. Genuine artisans built the lobby staircase from scratch, using just a single surviving newel post as their guide. Ornately crafted woodwork can be found throughout the inn. The downstairs lobby, restaurant, and bar are finished in cypress. Adirondack rockers sit on the wraparound verandas. My favorite room, the bar, has a grand, nautical feel to it, as if it belonged on the *Titanic.* Just two weeks after the Gibson reopened in November 1985, Hurricane Kate slammed Florida's Panhandle. Undaunted, the Kouns kept the bar open and threw a Key Largo–style hurricane party. Humphrey Bogart would have approved.

Wakulla Springs

Wakulla Springs is the largest and deepest spring in the world. Its waters are so clear that the bottom, 185 feet down, can be seen from the surface. Universal Studios chose Wakulla Springs to film the 1954 sci-fi/horror classic *The Creature from the Black Lagoon* because of its exceptionally clear waters. It has also been the site of numerous archeological excavations. Divers discovered a complete mastodon skeleton at the bottom of the springs in 1935. The reconstructed mastodon now stands in the Museum of Florida History in Tallahassee.

All manner of wildlife thrives in the park: Alligators, deer, raccoons, and even a few bears live there.

Wakulla Springs Lodge
Edward Ball/Wakulla Springs State Park
550 Wakulla Park Drive
Wakulla Springs 32327
(850) 926-0700
www.floridastateparks.org/wakullasprings/default.cfm

Edward Ball was the brother-in-law of Alfred I. DuPont, as well as the executor and trustee of DuPont's sizable estate and trust. Ball built a banking, telephone, railroad, and paper-and-box-manufacturing empire out of the trust, worth an estimated $33 million in 1935 when DuPont died. Ball had grown that into more than $2 billion by the time he passed away in 1981 at age ninety-three.

One of Edward Ball's proudest achievements was the construction of the Wakulla Springs Lodge in 1937. The twenty-seven-room lodge is essentially the same today as it was in the 1930s. Ball insisted that it always continue to reflect that era, and he also insisted that it never become so exclusive that it would not be affordable to "common folks."

Wakulla Springs Lodge reminds me of a palatial Spanish hacienda. The first thing that caught my eye when I walked into the lobby was the cypress ceiling beams with hand-painted Aztec designs on them. Blue and gold Spanish tiles frame the entranceway. The floors are mauve, red, and gray Tennessee marble tiles in a checkerboard pattern. A giant fireplace, made from native limestone and trimmed in marble, dominates the far wall. The most intriguing thing sits in a glass case at one end of the lobby: the stuffed and mounted remains of Old Joe, an eleven-foot-long alligator.

Old Joe was first spotted at the springs in the mid-1930s while the lodge was being built. For three decades, he was a Wakulla Springs fixture that had gained a reputation as a docile old gator that never bothered anyone. In 1966, however, he was shot and killed. Carl

WAKULLA SPRINGS LODGE

Buchheister, then-president of the Audubon Society, offered a $5,000 reward for information leading to the arrest of the gunman, but no one was ever caught. Old Joe's plaque reads, "Old Joe's first and only cage." Just past Old Joe is the soda fountain shop. There is no bar in the Wakulla Springs Lodge. Instead, Ball, who was fond of ginger whips (ice cream, ginger ale, and whipped cream), had a sixty-foot-long, solid-marble soda fountain counter installed.

The lodge and grounds sit on the north bank of the springs. From the top of the twenty-foot-high diving platform, you can look down on bream and bass schooling on the bottom. The water is amazingly clear. It's no wonder that Hollywood chose Wakulla Springs to film the *Tarzan* features and movies like *Around the World Under the Sea* and *Airport 77* in addition to *The Creature from the Black Lagoon.*

STEINHATCHEE

Longtime friends Michael and Leslie Poole introduced me to the sleepy Florida Big Bend fishing village of Steinhatchee. Along with their two sons, Blake and Preston, they have been making annual scalloping and fishing trips there for many years. Fishing, boating, and scalloping on the grass flats of the bay at the mouth of the river are Steinhatchee's prime attractions. Pronounced Steen-hat-chee, the name means "dead man's river" in the Creek language.

Steinhatchee Landing Resort
203 Ryland Circle
Highway 51 North
Steinhatchee 32359
(352) 498-3513
(800) 584-1709
www.steinhatcheelanding.com

A couple of miles upriver from town, along the north bank, you'll find Steinhatchee Landing Resort, a nature-conscious village with oak- and magnolia-shaded lanes and Florida Cracker style homes.

Georgia developers Dean and Loretta Fowler began building the village in 1990. Dean first arrived in Taylor County, Florida, in the late 1980s for a weekend fishing expedition at the invitation of a group of banker friends.

In his gentle Georgia accent, Dean told me, "I fell in love with the river and this rustic fishing village town and decided to build a vacation home here. Before long, Loretta and I were spending the majority of our spare time here. It occurred to me that it was mostly Georgia men who would come here to fish. They rarely brought their families because there wasn't much for families to do. I started thinking about

STEINHATCHEE LANDING RESORT

what families would enjoy doing here. Then I started a scratch-pad list that evolved into the idea of a resort complex with the right amenities to attract families."

Dean had built nursing homes and retirement developments in Georgia, so he knew what a project like this entailed.

"Condominium cracker boxes just wouldn't look right in this rustic little town," Dean explained, "so I called the University of Florida School of Architecture to see if they had an expert in vintage Florida architecture. They introduced me to Professor Ron Haase, who had written a book called *Classic Cracker: Florida's Wood-Frame Vernacular Architecture* (Pineapple Press). Ron came up with the design criteria. He designed the first nine houses and the restaurant. Other architects have designed houses, but they follow the guidelines laid out by Ron."

CEDAR KEY

It's probably fair to compare today's Cedar Key to the Key West of sixty years ago. The whiff of salt and fish is always in the air. No one is in a hurry. Except during festival weekends, this is a much quieter place than it was a century ago. Although the town is called Cedar Key, it's actually on Way Key, once a "way" station for sailing vessels to resupply and drop ballast. It's also fair to describe Cedar Key as "way" out there—geographically, artistically, and attitudinally.

As in many Florida towns, a railroad brought commerce to Cedar Key. Florida's first cross-state railroad, the Atlantic to Gulf/Florida Railroad Company Line completed in 1861, ran from Fernandina to Cedar Key. Cedar milling was the dominant industry in Cedar Key from the 1870s through the 1890s. Pencil manufacturer A.W. Faber had a mill on Atsena Otie Key, half a mile offshore. Naturally, seafood has always figured prominently in Cedar Key's economy. Today this area is the largest producer of farm-raised clams in the country.

The drive down Highway 24 from Otter Creek to Cedar Key is long and straight. If you're traveling it on the third weekend in October or the third weekend in April, you'll likely run into a traffic jam miles before you reach town. Cedar Key's Seafood Festival (October) and Old Florida Arts Festival (April) are two of the oldest and most popular such events in the state. They're terrific festivals, but don't expect to see much of the town or soak up its offbeat character while they're going on. Any other time you'll probably have the highway to yourself, and the most traffic you'll encounter in town will be a bicycle or an occasional old pickup truck on Second Street. Cedar Key moves at an unhurried pace, dictated mostly by whim or weather, hence its quirky charm.

Cedar Key can claim some famous visitors. Naturalist John Muir finished his thousand-mile walk from Indiana to the Gulf of Mexico in 1867. He had contracted malaria and spent months recuperating in Cedar Key. Writer Pearl Buck and singer Tennessee Ernie Ford have stayed at the Island Hotel. The visitor everyone likes to talk about, however, is Jimmy Buffet, who played in the Neptune Bar at the Island Hotel, way back when he got airtime only on country stations.

Cedar Key Bed & Breakfast
810 Third Street
Cedar Key 32625
(352) 543-9000
www.cedarkeybandb.com

Only a three-block stroll from downtown Cedar Key and two blocks from the Gulf, the Cedar Key Bed & Breakfast occupies the historic, tin-roofed, two-story Wadley House. The Eagle Cedar Mill Company built the house as an employee residence in 1880, at the height of Cedar Key's cedar harvesting boom. For a while, the daughter of David Yulee, Florida's first U.S. Senator who also built the Atlantic to Gulf/Florida Railroad, operated a boarding house here. In 1919 it was purchased by B.C. Wadley and remained in his family until 1991.

Richard and Brenda Pancake purchased house and remodeled it into a bed-and-breakfast in 1992. Then in 1994, Lois Benninghoff and Bob Davenport bought and expanded it by adding on to the back and cultivating a garden courtyard adjacent to the house. Current owners Bill and Alice Phillips purchased it in 2003. The main house has six rooms plus a one-room Honeymoon Cottage. New additions include a one-bedroom suite behind the main house and a two-bedroom suite a mile away in a house overlooking the Gulf.

CEDAR KEY BED & BREAKFAST

Cedar Key Harbour Master Suites
390 Dock Street
Cedar Key 32625
(352) 543-9146
www.cedarkeyharbourmaster.com

It would be easy to miss the Cedar Key Harbour Master Suites, housed above the Dilly Dally Gally gift shop, where the inn's registration desk is. The inn has nine spacious and comfortably furnished suites with full kitchens, king-size beds, and private balconies, most with views of

CEDAR KEY HARBOUR MASTER SUITES

the Gulf of Mexico. The third-floor, two-bedroom penthouse Sea Pearl Suite is the highest point on Dock Street and offers a panoramic view.

Island Hotel
373 Second Street
Cedar Key 32625
(352) 543-5111
(800) 432-4640
www.islandhotel-cedarkey.com

Cedar Key's most famous landmark, the Island Hotel, has survived ravaging hurricanes, floods, fires, and the Civil War. It was constructed with oak beams, hand-cut wooden floors and interior walls, and twelve-inch-thick, tabby exterior walls. I've looked at ninety-year-old photos of the hotel at the Cedar Key Historical Society Museum, and it looks just the same today.

The Island Hotel was built in 1859 as Parsons and Hale's General Store. When Union troops invaded the town during the Civil War, they burned most of the buildings but left the store standing because they needed it to store supplies and house troops. No doubt this was a frustrating time for owner Major John Parsons, who commanded a detachment of Confederate volunteers.

Following the war, Parsons and his partner, Francis Hale, reopened the general store. Famous naturalist John Muir described the store in his 1867 journal entry: "I stepped into a little store, which had a considerable trade in quinine, and alligator and rattlesnake skins. . . ." Sometime in the 1880s, Parsons and Hale began taking boarders and serving meals. In 1896, before hurricanes were assigned names, a furious hurricane hit Cedar Key, devastating most of it but leaving the store intact. Most historians mark the 1896 hurricane as the end of Cedar Key's prosperous industrial period.

Property investor Simon Feinberg bought the building in 1915 and remodeled it as the Bay Hotel. A second-floor veranda that wraps around two sides of the hotel was added during his tenure. In the years that followed, the hotel changed names and owners frequently. During the Great Depression, one owner tried to burn it down three times, but the fire department was just across the street and always managed to save it.

Everyone seems to agree that the hotel's heyday began in 1946, when Bessie and Loyal Gibbs bought it and renamed it the Island Hotel. The previous owners had operated a brothel out of the place, and it had become quite run-down. Bessie and Loyal toiled exhaustively to put the hotel back in shape. Gibby ran the bar and Bessie ran the restaurant. In 1948 they hired artist Helen Tooker to paint the picture of King Neptune that still hangs behind the bar in the hotel's Neptune Lounge. That painting, like the hotel, seems to be blessed with multiple lives. It has survived gunshots and hurricanes, even flooding when a 1950 hurricane tore off part of the Island Hotel's roof. Bessie's

VIEW FROM UPSTAIRS PORCH OF THE ISLAND HOTEL

culinary skills and panache with the clientele, plus Loyal's friendliness at the bar, won them popularity and customers. Loyal died in 1962, and Bessie, while still operating the hotel, went on to become Cedar Key's mayor from 1967–1968. She started the very popular annual Arts and Crafts Festival and was also instrumental in opening the Cedar Key Historical Society Museum. With her health deteriorating, she sold the Island Hotel in 1974 and died tragically in a house fire the following year. Known for its native Florida seafood dishes, like soft-shell blue crab, the Island Hotel's restaurant is especially known for its hearts of palm salad, Bessie's most famous recipe.

The Island Hotel is certainly rustic, with well-weathered wood and some cracked plaster on its exterior, but that's all integral to its old-Florida charm. In 2004 Andy and Stanley Bair purchased the hotel. The husband-and-wife team had previously operated an inn on Andros Island in the Bahamas. The Bairs' first job was to repaint, repair, and add new furniture. I was happy to see that they did so without changing the character of the place. My room, number 23, was quaint and charming. I found it exceedingly comfortable and nicely furnished with antiques. It has a claw-foot tub with a wraparound curtain, making it into a shower. Out on the upstairs veranda, I found a comfy bench swing overlooking Second Street, the perfect place to relax and read a book.

Every old hotel has its ghost stories, and the Island Hotel has plenty. Some think previous owner Simon Feinberg is still there. Others have reported seeing the apparition of a Confederate soldier. Perhaps the most intriguing story has to do with room 29, a corner room upstairs where Bessie Gibbs used to stay. Furniture is rearranged and pictures are moved on the walls. During my stay, I woke up at 3:00 A.M. and decided to wander the halls and shoot a few pictures. Room 29 was unoccupied and the door was unlocked, so I nervously peeked in. I didn't see anything, but I quietly apologized to Bessie in case I disturbed her.

NORTHEAST

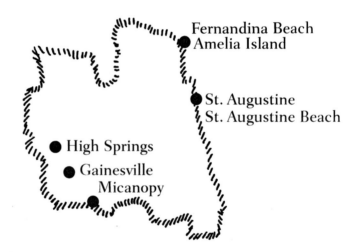

Fernandina Beach
Amelia Island

St. Augustine
St. Augustine Beach

High Springs

Gainesville
Micanopy

FERNANDINA BEACH, AMELIA ISLAND

Amelia Island's history is as rich as that of any location in Florida. Eight different countries' flags have flown over the island—more than any other place in the United States.

Fernandina Beach, on the north end of Amelia Island, became a thriving community in the mid-1800s with the arrival of the railroad. Despite its name, the main commercial and residential districts are not on the beach but on the Intracoastal Waterway side. Originally, the town was located just north of its present location. Railroad owner David Yulee promised the town's residents prosperity if they would agree to move the community about a mile south, closer to his railroad terminus and port on the Amelia River. They agreed, and Fernandina's golden era began. In a short time, luxury steamers from the North began carrying wealthy vacationers to Amelia Island. Elegant inns and palatial Victorian mansions went up on the streets north and south of Centre Street. Fernandina also became a vital shipping port, and the town boomed. The Spanish-American War in 1898 generated even more shipping and rail business. Not only had Yulee kept his promise, but the results of his efforts exceeded everyone's expectations. For nearly fifty years, Fernandina was both a world-renowned resort and a center of commerce. Then, at the turn of the century, Henry Flagler chose not to connect his railroad to Yulee's railroad line, bypassing Amelia Island and diverting passengers to St. Augustine and Flagler's Ponce de Leon Hotel. Fernandina's flourish fizzled almost as rapidly as it had begun.

The good news is that most of the Victorian structures survived the subsequent decades. In 1973 downtown Fernandina Beach received designation as a historic district from the National Register of Historic Places. In 1987 the historic district was expanded to encompass about fifty blocks. In 1977 Fernandina began renovating historic Centre Street. Other Florida small towns have done similar work in more recent years, but Fernandina was one of the first and continues the process even today.

Addison on Amelia Bed & Breakfast
614 Ash Street
Fernandina Beach 32034
(904) 277-1604
(800) 943-1804
www.addisononamelia.com

Three houses comprise Addison on Amelia, located in Fernandina's historic Victorian neighborhood and unofficial bed-and-breakfast district south of Centre Street. The original house was built in 1876 for local merchant Frank Simmons. The other two are new structures built in 1996 and are perfect architectural matches with the original house. All three surround a lush garden courtyard with brick walkways and a fountain centerpiece.

In all there are fourteen rooms numbered 1 through 15. (There is no room 13.). Most have whirlpool baths, and some have canopied and four-poster beds. My room, number 12, overlooked the courtyard. It was roomy and quite comfortable and had the largest bathtub I have ever seen in a bed-and-breakfast. Breakfast, by the way, is a gourmet event with a variety of choices each morning. I had French toast made from croissants. Delectable.

Bob and Shannon Tidball have owned the Addison since 2007, and they were gracious hosts during my stay. Bob and daughter Lee served us wine and cheese at 5:00 P.M., happy hour, the perfect time to meet other guests and trade recommendations for favorite restaurants. Bob suggested we try España, a family-operated Portuguese restaurant just two blocks away. Outstanding recommendation. It's now one of my top five Florida restaurants.

I asked Bob about the Addison's distinctive mint green exterior color, and he told me that it is actually Sherwin-Williams' Greensleeves. "I keep dozens of cans of it," he said. Since the house is a historic structure, the color had to be approved by Fernandina's historical

ADDISON ON AMELIA BED & BREAKFAST (Mary Ellen Connelly)

commission. Bob explained that keeping the historic house (and the new additions) painted and properly maintained is a perpetual process. In fact, Bob was painting when I arrived, and the Addison is in impeccable shape.

A relaxed and carefree stay is a priority at the Addison. The Tidballs are happy to make arrangements for anything from carriage rides to historical tours, and they have their own fleet of cruiser bicycles, along with beach chairs and umbrellas, all complimentary for guests.

During happy hour, one of the guests asked Bob about an Addison ghost story he had heard. Bob admitted that he is a skeptic but that on occasion peculiar things have happened in room 4. Apparently some think that the ghost of a mischievous young boy likes to turn the alarm clock on at odd hours.

Amelia Island Williams House Bed & Breakfast
103 South Ninth Street
Fernandina Beach 32034
(904) 277-2328
(800) 414-9258
www.williamshouse.com

The Amelia Island Williams House, built in 1856, is named for surveyor Marcellus Williams, who purchased it in 1859. The Williams family remained in the house for a century, except for one interruption: Union troops took over Fernandina for a while during the Civil War, and Williams moved his family to central Florida during the occupation. The Union army used the house as an infirmary during that time.

Antebellum Folk-Victorian best describes the style of the Williams House. Elaborate gingerbread-design porch columns (added to the house in 1880 and designed by Robert Schuyler, the New York architect who designed the Fairbanks House) are its signature motif. An ornate, wrought iron fence surrounds the property. In 1993 Dick Flitz and Chris Carter bought the house and turned it into a bed-and-breakfast. Current owners Bryon and Deborah McCutchen purchased it from them. There are five rooms in the main house and five more in the adjacent Hearthstone Cottage and Carriage House.

Amelia Oceanfront Bed & Breakfast
584 South Fletcher Avenue
Fernandina Beach 32034
(904) 430-0026
www.ameliaoceanfrontbb.com

Walter Nolan Baker, a regional sales manager for a tire company, and his third wife, Lucille, built this beachfront house as their residence in 1938. After Baker died in 1944, Lucille married William Veech, who eventually began renting the upstairs rooms as apartments. In 1981 David and Susan Caples (now owners of Elizabeth Pointe Lodge) purchased the house, renovated it, and opened it as a bed-and-

AMELIA OCEAN-
FRONT BED &
BREAKFAST

breakfast. Subsequent owners did more remodeling in 2000 and 2010, including the addition of the mermaid fountain that sits out front. Current owners Han Ramakers and his wife, T.J. Seaton, bought the inn in 2012 and are doing a superb job of maintaining the inn's historic charm. All six rooms are suites with sitting areas and kitchenettes, decorated in a comfortable, beach-cottage style.

Blue Heron Inn Bed & Breakfast
102 South Seventh Street
Fernandina Beach 32034
(904) 445-9034
www.ameliaislandblueheroninn.com

The Blue Heron is an intimate, circa-1904 bed-and-breakfast in Fernandina's "bed-and-breakfast district" neighborhood. It has just six rooms—all with king-size beds—and a heated swimming pool.

BLUE HERON INN BED & BREAKFAST

Elizabeth Pointe Lodge
98 South Fletcher Avenue
Fernandina Beach 32034
(904) 277-4851
www.elizabethpointlodge.com

Elizabeth Pointe's main lodge may resemble a grand, old mansion you might find on Cape Cod, with its shingle sides and gambrel roof, but it was actually built in 1992. A stand of sea oats on a low bluff are all that separate it from the wide beach and the Atlantic Ocean. There are twenty rooms in the main lodge and five more in the adjacent Ocean House and Miller Cottage.

The main lodge sits on stilts, so the lobby, breakfast room, and library/sitting room are actually on the second floor. The decor here is distinctly New England nautical, particularly in the lobby, with its huge stone fireplace, wicker chairs with over-stuffed cushions, and library

ELIZABETH POINTE LODGE

shelves filled with books. Panoramic windows offer a spectacular sunset view.

I stayed in the ocean-facing upstairs suite in the Ocean House, with its own patio and a boardwalk that leads through the sand dunes to the beach.

Fairbanks House Bed & Breakfast
227 South Seventh Street
Fernandina Beach 32034
(904) 277-0500
(888) 891-9880
www.fairbankshouse.com

Bill and Theresa Hamilton spent ten years kicking the owning a bed-and-breakfast idea around before they landed in Fernandina Beach.

The Fairbanks House was not for sale when they found it. They point out that the advantage of looking at properties that aren't currently for sale is that you're more apt to be looking at ones that are in tip-top shape. Nelson and Mary Smelker had owned and operated the Fairbanks House for about three years (its units had been rented out as apartments prior to that) when Bill and Theresa came along in 1997.

"The Smelkers did an extraordinary job with this place," Theresa told me. "Mary Smelker did every bit of the decorating that you see. She made the bedspreads, the window treatments. She reupholstered the furniture with matching fabrics." The Smelkers also did extensive remodeling and landscaping. They added a swimming pool, a parking area, and additional bathrooms; plus they purchased three adjacent cottages and added them to the inn.

It met all of Bill and Theresa's criteria, and it was fully operational. "We were charmed," adds Theresa, "by both the Fairbanks House and the town of Fernandina, a wonderful place filled with genuinely friendly people. We fell in love with all of it."

FAIRBANKS HOUSE BED & BREAKFAST

The Fairbanks House is a colossal, three-story (four when you include the tower) Italianate estate. It is considered by many people to be the finest and best-preserved example of Italianate architecture in Florida. It has all of the identifying characteristics of that nineteenth-century style: tall, narrow windows (some with arches); decorative roof eaves and brackets; decorative porch columns; elaborately detailed molding and trim; ornate brick chimneys; and, of course, a tower. There are ten fireplaces. Tiles that depict Shakespearean characters frame the living room fireplace, and the dining room fireplace tiles depict *Aesop's Fables* characters. The floors are heart of pine, and the grand staircase is made of Honduran mahogany.

The grounds take up half of the block between Beech and Cedar

Streets. The inn consists of eleven rooms, including two suites and three cottages. The Tower Suite on the third floor has two bedrooms, a living room, and a kitchen. A ladder leads up into the fifteen-foot-high, glass-enclosed, air-conditioned tower, which is furnished with an antique French game table and chairs. Of course, the best thing is the view across the rooftops in Fernandina's Victorian neighborhood.

George Rainsford Fairbanks was a Confederate major, a former state senator, a historian, an educator, and one of the founders of the University of the South in Sewanee, Tennessee. He was lured to Fernandina in 1879 by railroad magnate and then-Senator David Yulee to run Fernandina's *Florida Mirror* newspaper.

Fairbanks built his house, the town's most extravagant residence, in 1885, at the height of Fernandina's golden era. He commissioned the home's design to famous architect Robert Schuyler. It had indoor plumbing, a telephone, a cistern for collecting rain water, and a dumbwaiter for lifting firewood from the basement to the upper floors. Yes, the Fairbanks House has a basement, a Florida rarity.

Local lore claims that Fairbanks had built the house as a surprise for his wife. Reportedly Mrs. Fairbanks was not pleasantly surprised. "Too ostentatious," she was rumored to have proclaimed, and the house became known as Fairbanks' Folly.

I stayed in one of the cottages, a quaint one-bedroom with a king-size bed, a kitchenette, and a bathroom with both a shower and a Jacuzzi. Breakfast at the Fairbanks House is a marvelous treat. On the veranda overlooking the pool, we feasted on banana sorbet with kiwi fruit sauce and orange-pecan French toast.

Upkeep of these historic homes is a perpetual task, and when I visited in 2012, the Fairbanks House was in the midst of an exterior repaint and remodel.

Florida House Inn
22 South Third Street
Fernandina Beach 32034
(904) 491-3322
www.floridahouseinn.com

The Florida House is the state's oldest operating inn. Built in 1857 by David Yulee's Florida Railroad Company, the house was used as a barracks by occupying Union troops during the Civil War. After the war, the Florida House Inn was purchased by an army major who had been stationed at Fort Clinch, on the north tip of Amelia Island. Over the decades, the inn's guest list of dignitaries has included various Carnegies, Rockefellers, and DuPonts; Henry Ford; José Martí; and even Stan Laurel and Oliver Hardy.

I stayed at the inn in 1998, after then-owners Bob and Karen Warner had done considerable restoration work. It had a comfortable, rustic atmosphere, and dinner was home-cooked Southern food served family style at large tables. Subsequently the Warners sold it, and in 2009 the inn fell on difficult times, ultimately closing in January 2010. Jacksonville banker Ernest Saltmarsh, who had vacation property on Amelia Island and had always admired the inn, bought it and immediately began another major renovation. Emily Sands, Saltmarsh's daughter, and her husband, Marshal, operate the inn, which reopened in December 2010. In 2012 Emily gave me a tour of the inn, which has seventeen rooms that are freshly painted and furnished with period antiques. Emily and her family completely remodeled the dining room and the bar, removing walls to open up and brighten the space. They also re-landscaped the grounds in the back and added an outdoor wedding and reception area on the side. In all, the Florida House Inn's makeover is impressive.

FLORIDA HOUSE INN

Hoyt House Bed & Breakfast
804 Atlantic Avenue
Fernandina Beach 32034
(904) 277-4300
(800) 432-2085
www.hoythouse.com

Banker Fred Hoyt built this grand, three-story Victorian as his residence in 1905. Hoyt House has ten elegantly decorated rooms, plus something a little unusual: a thirty-nine-foot yacht that doubles as guest quarters. Hoyt House's sprawling grounds give guests lots of space to relax and plenty of amenities, such as hammocks, a gazebo, a hot tub, and a heated swimming pool.

HOYT HOUSE BED & BREAKFAST

HIGH SPRINGS

High Springs sits near the confluence of some of north central Florida's most beautiful springs and rivers. The Santa Fe and Ichetucknee Rivers, Poe Springs, Blue Springs, and Ginnie Springs are all close by. For canoeists, kayakers, tubers, scuba divers, and cave divers, it's the ideal bivouac. It's also an interesting place to visit for nonaquatic types. Downtown High Springs' selection of antiques shops draws day and weekend visitors from around the state.

Grady House Bed & Breakfast
420 North West 1st Avenue
High Springs 32643
(386) 454-2206
www.gradyhouse.com

From the sidewalk on First Avenue, the 1917 Grady House appears as a charming, two-story Arts and Crafts bungalow. The inviting front porch, with its twin gable roof, is furnished with wicker chairs and a bench swing at one end. What you don't see from the sidewalk are the lush and extensive backyard gardens, with winding brick pathways, fountains, a koi pond, and a gazebo—a genuine secret garden.

The main house has five rooms, each named for its color theme: the Yellow Room, the Peach Room, the Green Room (overlooking the gardens), the Navy Room (with a nautical theme and a sitting room with a daybed), and the Red Room (decorated with paintings and lithographs of classical nudes). All of the rooms are filled with early twentieth-century antiques. Some have claw-foot tubs and sitting rooms. The living room and dining room continue the warm, early-bungalow ambience. Next door is the 1896 Easterlin House, which they call Skeet's Cottage, which has two large bedrooms and a bath, ideal for a family. It all feels very much like someone's grandmother's

GRADY HOUSE BED & BREAKFAST

house—except for the nudes in the Red Room.

I stayed in the bright and cheerful Yellow Room. Owner Lucie Regensdorf served us a magnificent breakfast that began with fresh strawberries, blueberries, blackberries, and two kinds of coffee cake. I assumed that was the entire breakfast and had filled up nicely, and then she brought out sausage, egg, and potato strata with smoked bacon and buttermilk biscuits!

Lucie and Paul Regensdorf purchased the Grady House in 2006 from Tony Boothby and Kirk Eppenstein, who remodeled the house into a bed-and-breakfast in 1998. It had previously been a bakery, a boarding house, and an apartment house. Lucie and Paul have maintained the houses and grounds in immaculate condition. It's their home too, along with their four rescued Dalmatians.

Rustic Inn Bed & Breakfast Inn
15529 North West State Road 45
High Springs 32643
(386) 454-1223
www.rusticinn.net

Two miles south of downtown High Springs, in rolling pastureland, the Rustic Inn sits unobtrusively among gentlemen's horse farms, which it once was. A white pasture fence lines the front of the seven-acre property. There is an existing horse pasture adjacent to the inn and a forest of pine trees with a hiking path behind it. In its previous life, the six-room inn was the horse stable, although it has been so extensively remodeled that you would never recognize it as such.

Each of the rooms has a different theme that relates to animals or nature: the Cat Room, the Zebra Room, the Panda Room, the Everglades Room, the Tropical Room, and the Sea Mammals Room. I stayed in the Cat Room, one of the two end rooms, each of which has a large picture window. The Cat Room's theme is mostly leopards:

leopard wallpaper, leopard-print shower curtain, and a jungle scene comforter with—you guessed it—leopards. Beautiful framed prints of leopards and tigers hang on the walls, along with a "Save the Florida Panther" poster that features a beautiful photo taken by photographer Burton McNeely.

GAINESVILLE

The university town of Gainesville developed in the mid- and late-1800s as a crossroads for three major Florida industries: citrus farming, phosphate mining, and lumber harvesting. In 1920 the Atlantic Coast Line Railroad ran down the center of West Main Street. As the University of Florida grew, the town's economic focus shifted to academia. Florida's largest and oldest university, the University of Florida traces its roots back to East Florida Seminary in Ocala in 1853. The Seminary moved to Gainesville in 1866 and subsequently consolidated with Florida Agricultural College, eventually leading to the establishment of the university in 1906.

Camellia Rose Inn
205 South East Seventh Street
Gainesville 32601
(352) 395-7673
www.camelliaroseinn.com

Pat and Tom McCants were first drawn to Gainesville's historic bed-and-breakfast district by relatives Joe and Cindy Montalto, who own Magnolia Plantation. In 2006 they found what they were looking for just one block away: a two-story Queen Anne built by Gainesville

CAMELLIA ROSE INN

automobile dealer Thomas Swearington in 1903. Camellia Rose Inn has six rooms in the main house—four with their own fireplace—plus a two-room cottage, Spat's Hideaway, with its own kitchenette.

Laurel Oak Inn
221 South East Seventh Street
Gainesville 32601
(352) 373-4535
(877) 373-4535
www.laureloakinn.com

This 1885 Queen Anne Victorian was a summer house for residents Wilburn and Fanny Lassiter. Subsequent owners in the 1920s divided the house into apartments. Through the 1960s and 1970s, like

LAUREL OAK INN

others in this district, it was a college boarding house. (The current owners think Gainesville native Tom Petty may have lived there for a while.) It underwent a partial renovation in the early 1990s. Then in 1999, Monta and Peggy Burt purchased it, spent the next two years completing the renovations, and turned it into their bed-and-breakfast, the Laurel Oak Inn. The inn has five rooms furnished and decorated in turn-of-the-century style, each with either a fireplace or gas stove.

Magnolia Plantation
309 South East Seventh Street
Gainesville 32601
(352) 375-6653
(800) 201-2379
www.magnoliabnb.com

Joe and Cindy Montalto definitely had their work cut out for them when they took on the task of converting a college "animal house" into an elegant bed-and-breakfast. What they found beneath the layers of rubble was a rare architectural jewel.

Victorian French Second Empire architecture was in vogue in the United States from 1860 to about 1890. During his administration, President Ulysses S. Grant commissioned the construction of many public buildings in the style. It caught on as a fashionable trend in houses too, more so in the Northeast. Grant built his own house in French Second Empire, and it even became known as General Grant style, which is why it didn't catch on in the South.

One recognizable element of a French Second Empire house is its steep mansard roof, named after French seventeenth-century architect Francois Mansart. Remember the Addams Family house? That's French Second Empire. Restored or well-preserved examples of the style are extremely rare in the South, but a shining exception is Magnolia Plantation in Gainesville's historic bed-and-breakfast district.

In 1990 Joe and Cindy Montalto bought what had been a student boarding house in need of a lot of work. "The place looked rough," Cindy told me. "It was filled with trash. Plaster was falling off the walls. Joe sanded all the floors. I stripped all the woodwork. We pulled the walls down ourselves. It was a complete gut and redo." It took them until May 1991 to open, and the results of their labor are astonishing. Magnolia Plantation ranks among the most meticulous and detailed restorations I've seen.

MAGNOLIA PLANTATION

Dudley Williams, who worked in the local lumber industry, and his wife, Melinza, built the house in 1885. Prominent businessman Emmett Baird bought it in 1890. The Bairds owned one of the largest wholesale hardware store chains in Florida at the turn of the century, and they founded the first bank in Gainesville. They also built an opera house and owned a livery stable. Ownership of the house remained in the Baird family until 1960.

The house has eleven-foot ceilings and heart pine floors and is full of original details, like the corner dust plates on the staircase. There are ten fireplaces, all original. In order to retain the original design and dimensions of each room yet give each room its own bathroom, the Montaltos did something very clever. A claw-foot tub with wraparound curtains occupies a corner or nook inside each bedroom apart from the bathroom. In two of the rooms they actually built bathrooms, or water closets, from the original closets. "You can take a shower, and then step out in front of the fireplace to dry off," Cindy points out.

One of my favorite rooms is the Gardenia Room, which Cindy calls the "fluffy room." It has an Eastlake double bed that's as old as the house, and it has one of the water closets. Its bay window overlooks the gardens of the Secret Garden House next door.

Double-glass doors lead into the largest room, the Magnolia Room, which was the Bairds' master bedroom. A long lounging chair with an elevated headrest sits at the foot of the queen-size bed. Cindy explained that it's called a "fainting couch." "Back then the women wore corsets, and they were so tight that they couldn't breathe, so they had to have some place to lie down and faint!"

On the outside of the house, Joe and Cindy have continued their obsession with authentic details. The mansard roof has its original fish-scale slate shingles. The flat top of the roof is the original tin. Characteristic of this style of architecture, there are intricately carved roof cornice brackets, tall bracketed windows, and a double front door with a stained glass window above. A four-story tower with an iron-railed cupola on top rises above the entrance. Cindy and Joe chose different colors to emphasize all of the trim details, gingerbread, and bracketing—and there's lots of it. "It is an ongoing painting project," Cindy said. "We do a side of the house each year. Our painters call it the 'paint-by-numbers house.' They're the only ones who know all the exact colors."

Magnolia Plantation's pastoral grounds include brick pathways that wind among oak and pine trees and past flower beds, a pond, a gazebo, and a fountain, all with the dreamlike quality of an idyllic English garden. Joe and his father did most of the work themselves, including laying the brick pathways.

In addition to the main house, Joe and Cindy have included a 1950s duplex next door, which they call the Secret Garden House. They completely remodeled both units, expanding the kitchens/ sunrooms out onto enclosed porches with Mexican tile floors. Each has two bedrooms, a queen-size bed in one and two twins in the other.

Next door, on the opposite side of the main house, is Miss Huey's Cottage, a Cracker house built in the 1870s. Miss Huey was a Shands Hospital nurse who took care of handicapped babies. She lived in the house from 1960 until she passed away in 1994. According to deed records, the house was moved to the spot in 1930 from its original site on Main Street. The original deed indicates that it was a "house of colored rental," which means that it was probably a freed slave's home. Joe and Cindy bought it in 1994 and applied their finely honed restoration skills. It has rocking chair porches both in front and in back. The tin-roofed rear porch overlooks more gardens and a fountain where an elephant spews water from its trunk, all shaded by a three-hundred-year-old live oak. Miss Huey's Cottage has two bedrooms with one queen-size and one double bed, a kitchenette, and a living room with a fireplace, over which Miss Huey's portrait hangs on the wall.

There is a local legend that Emmett Baird found pirate treasure buried on the banks of the Suwannee River in the late 1800s. The remains were supposedly hidden in his house sometime prior to his death in the 1920s. The Montaltos are adamant that there is no hidden booty. They certainly would have uncovered it during their thorough renovation. Boy, they sure did one heck of a nice restoration, though!

Sweetwater Branch Inn Bed and Breakfast
625 East University Avenue
Gainesville 32601
(352) 373-6760
(800) 595-7760
www.sweetwaterinn.com

The Sweetwater Branch Inn has evolved into more than just a bed-and-breakfast. With two houses and six cottages—a total of eighteen rooms—it is a substantial compound that occupies half a city block. With its large reception/banquet hall, the venue has a reputation as the perfect place for weddings and receptions in Gainesville. It is a beautiful setting for a wedding.

The two handsomely restored Victorian houses—the circa-1885 Cushman-Colson House and the circa-1895 McKenzie House—are Sweetwater Branch's centerpieces. Everything is surrounded by a full acre of gardens, gazebos, and fountains.

SWEETWATER BRANCH INN BED AND BREAKFAST

MICANOPY

According to the Micanopy Historical Society Museum, a town called Wanton's Trading Post was established there in 1821. That makes it Florida's second-oldest town and its oldest inland town. In 1835 the name officially changed to Micanopy after Seminole Chief Micanopy. Huge live oaks hang over its two-block-long main street, Cholokka Boulevard, which you might recognize from the 1991 Michael J. Fox movie, *Doc Hollywood*. Micanopy was the perfect double for the fictitious Southern town of Grady.

Micanopy dodged the modernization bullet back in the early 1960s when the Department of Transportation rerouted Highway 441 a couple miles east of town rather than through it. When I-75 was built a few years later, it too missed Micanopy by several miles to the west. As a result, Cholokka Boulevard and the dozen residential square blocks around it—all declared a National Register Historic District in 1983—seem frozen in time. Cholokka Boulevard's brick storefronts look virtually the same as in photographs taken a hundred years ago. Micanopy is a gem for curio shoppers, antiquers, and antiquarian book collectors, with more than a dozen distinctive shops.

Herlong Mansion Bed & Breakfast
402 North East Cholokka Boulevard
Micanopy 32667
(362) 466-3322
(800) 437-5664
www.herlong.com

The history of the Herlong Mansion reads like an Edgar Allen Poe story. It is a place so permeated with intrigue and mystery that you can feel it as you walk up the long brick sidewalk to the front door.

Zetty and Natalie Herlong moved to Natalie's family home in

HERLONG MANSION BED & BREAKFAST

Micanopy in 1907 after their Alabama lumber business was destroyed in a fire. Natalie's parents, the Simontons, had built what was originally a two-story, wood-frame farmhouse back in the 1840s. But the Herlongs wanted something a bit grander, so in 1909 they remodeled by actually constructing a brick mansion on top of and around the original.

The Herlongs restarted their lumber business in Micanopy and became prominent citrus farmers as well. When Natalie passed away in 1950, her six children inherited equal shares of the house, and a contentious eighteen-year battle for sole ownership ensued. Eventually one sister, Inez, acquired legal possession of the house. On the very first day of her ownership, while cleaning in the second-floor bedroom that she and sister Mae had shared during childhood, Inez collapsed, went into a diabetic coma, and died shortly thereafter.

Over the years, guests and staff have reported the sound of footsteps or doors opening and closing upstairs when no one is there, usually in or around Mae's room. The Center for Paranormal Studies in Ocala has investigated the ghostly happenings several times and did report anomalous electromagnetic readings in the hallway on the second floor.

Stephen and Carolyn West were ready for a change of pace after owning and operating the Eaton Lodge in Key West for eleven years when they found the Herlong Mansion Bed & Breakfast for sale in 2006. The Wests added some of their own touch to the décor, with tropical artwork and light, airy drapes. "We wanted to make it a little brighter, more open air, and comfortable," Carolyn told me. In addition they re-landscaped and received a landscaping award from the Alachua County Tourist Development Board for their efforts.

In keeping with the Southern ambience, breakfast at the Herlong Mansion is a hearty affair. Expect Southern breakfast items like buttermilk biscuits, cheese grits, scrambled eggs, sausage, ham, and breakfast casseroles. I did stay upstairs but not in Inez and Mae's room. Mine faced the grand upstairs balcony that overlooks the front yard and Cholokka Boulevard—and nothing ghostly happened while I was there.

Micanopy is just twelve miles south of Gainesville, so on weekends when there are home football games at the University of Florida, the Herlong Mansion can be booked up to a year in advance. Adjacent to the house is the Herlong's separate banquet hall for weddings and conferences.

St. Augustine

When it comes to old and historic in Florida, you would be hard-pressed to find more of either anywhere other than in St. Augustine. Not only is this the oldest city in Florida, but it's also the oldest continuously occupied city in the United States.

Today St. Augustine is one of Florida's most popular destinations for vacationers and history buffs. Narrow avenues and alleyways interweave St. Augustine's historic district, bounded by the Matanzas River on the east and Flagler College on the west. The area was designated a National Landmark District by the National Park Service in 1970, and in 1983 more of the surrounding neighborhood was added as a National Register Historic District. Balconies hang out over the streets. Horse-drawn carriages clip-clop along the roads. It has the quaint look and feel of an old English village, not surprising since some of the older structures were built during British occupation from 1763 to 1784. St. George Street, which runs north to south through the center, is cordoned off for pedestrians. Antiques shops, gift shops, cafés, and bed-and-breakfasts now occupy many of the historic coquina and wooden buildings, some of which date back nearly three centuries.

On a visit in 2012, I found two outstanding little cafés worth mention down narrow, brick Aviles Street, a couple of blocks from the Casa Monica Hotel. La Herencia Café is an authentic Cuban café with mojo roast pork and black beans and rice as tasty as the best I've had in west Tampa. Two doors down, the Restaurant Café Sol Brasileirissimo serves mouth-watering Brazilian dishes. I had the feijoado completa, which is essentially everything in the kitchen: spicy beef, sausage, and smoked pork with black beans, rice, and shredded collards, topped with salsa and orange slices.

Agustin Inn
29 Cuna Street
St. Augustine 32084
(800) 248-7846
www.agustininn.com

The quaint, 1898 three-story Agustin Inn is situated off the beaten path on quiet, cobblestone Cuna Street. New owners bought the Agustin in 2010 and have done a thorough job of redecorating its eighteen rooms. The inn's tree-shaded front courtyard is a perfect, peaceful spot to enjoy coffee and breakfast in the morning.

Bayfront Marin House Bed & Breakfast
142 Avenida Menendez
St. Augustine 32084
(904) 824-4301
(866) 256-5887
www.bayfrontmarinhouse.com

Minorcan colony refugee Francisco Marin built the original house on this location sometime in the 1780s. In the 1890s, it was extensively enlarged by owner Captain Henry Belknap. Following the turn of the century, it continued to be added on to by various owners, and in 2003 it was completely restored and turned into a bed-and-breakfast. Overlooking Matanzas Bay, Bayfront Marin House is a luxuriously decorated fifteen-room inn in the oldest residential section of St. Augustine, south of King Street. Each of the rooms has a private outside entrance, and most have views of the bay as well as Jacuzzis. Pets are allowed in some rooms.

AGUSTIN INN

BAYFRONT MARIN HOUSE BED & BREAKFAST

Carriage Way Bed & Breakfast
70 Cuna Street
St. Augustine 32084
(904) 829-2467
(800) 908-9832
www.carriageway.com

Carriage Way, along the carriage route at the corner of Cuna and Cordova Streets, was built in 1883 by carpenter Edward Masters, who moved to St. Augustine to work on Henry Flagler's Ponce de Leon Hotel. The Johnson family has owned and operated the house as Carriage Way Bed & Breakfast since 1992. The main house has nine rooms, and there are two more in a cottage a couple of doors down.

CARRIAGE WAY BED & BREAKFAST

Casablanca Inn Bed & Breakfast
24 Avenida Menendez
St. Augustine 32084
(904) 829-0928
(800) 826-2626
www.casablancainn.com

Following the Prohibition Act of 1919, St. Augustine became a busy smuggling port. During the 1920s, the Casablanca was the circa-1914 Matanzas Hotel, and U.S. Treasury agents were regular patrons. An elderly woman, who remains anonymous, operated the Matanzas Hotel then and had an arrangement with smugglers—for a fee, of course—who were bringing their contraband into Matanzas Bay by night. If no agents were checked in to the hotel that evening, she would climb up onto the rooftop widow's walk and wave a lantern as an "all clear" signal. After fourteen years of Prohibition, this innkeeper reportedly died a wealthy woman. Legend claims that she can still be seen waving her lantern from the roof of what is now the Casablanca Inn.

There are twelve rooms in the main house on Avenida Menendez, plus eight rooms in the Coach House and three pet-friendly rooms in the Secret Garden Suites, all off Charlotte Street behind the main inn. Rooms 7 and 10, upstairs in the main inn, have private porches that overlook Matanzas Bay. I stayed in room 10, which has a fireplace and a comfy hammock on the porch. In keeping with tradition (and superstition), there is no room 13. Instead it's called room 00. A new addition is Casablanca's popular Tini Martini Bar with live jazz Friday and Saturday nights.

CASABLANCA INN BED & BREAKFAST

Casa de Solana
21 Aviles Street
St. Augustine 32084
(904) 824-3555
www.casadesolana.com

Don Manuel Lorenzo Solana built this home in St. Augustine's oldest

CASA DE SOLANA

residential section in 1763 out of coquina, just like Fort Castillo de San Marco. He added on to it in the early 1800s. Solana was one of the last remaining "mounted dragoons" of the Spanish Army in St. Augustine following British occupation. Casa de Solana has ten sumptuously decorated (and rumored to be haunted) rooms.

Casa de Suenos Bed & Breakfast
20 Cordova Street
St. Augustine 32084
(904) 824-0887
(800) 824-0804
www.casadesuenos.com

James Colee, a surveyor for Henry Flagler, built this house in 1904 across the street from his family's stagecoach and carriage business. It was originally a simple clapboard cottage, but in the 1920s, cigar manufacturer Patalina Carcaba purchased it and completely remodeled it into a Mediterranean/Spanish Eclectic style with varied-height flat roofs, parapet walls, and tall arched windows, an architectural style the house retains today.

When Ray and Sandy Tool bought the house in 1994, it was being used as an office building. It took the Tools a year to renovate, adding bathrooms (three with whirlpool tubs) and decorating lavishly to suit the Spanish style and the 1920s' era.

Kathleen Hurley purchased Casa de Suenos in 2001, and her first project was to redecorate its interior in a bright and contemporary style. Next she added upstairs balconies to two rooms and built a front-porch sunroom. The only downstairs room, called Nieves, has its own wheelchair-accessible ramp.

CASA DE SUENOS BED & BREAKFAST

Casa Monica Hotel
95 Cordova Street
St. Augustine 32084
(904) 827-1888
(888) 213-8903
www.casamonica.com

On January 1, 1888, Boston entrepreneur and architect Franklin Smith opened the Casa Monica Hotel on property that he had purchased from Henry Flagler. It was constructed at the same time and in the same architectural style—Spanish Renaissance with Moorish Revival elements—as Flagler's St. Augustine hotels: the Ponce de Leon (now Flagler College) and the Alcazar (now the Lightner Museum).

Less than four months after it opened, Flagler bought the hotel from Smith and renamed it the Cordova. In 1902 Flagler built a bridge between the Cordova and his Alcazar Hotel next door to make them one hotel.

Eventually the Cordova fell victim to the Great Depression. After it had been closed for three decades, St. Johns County bought the building in 1962 and, over the next two years, remodeled it into the St. Johns County Courthouse.

In 1997 Richard Kessler, central Florida hotelier and former CEO of Days Inns of America, bought the courthouse and spent two years on a complete restoration, bringing it back to its original Flagler-era splendor. He reopened it in 1999 with its original name, the Casa Monica Hotel, named for Saint Monica, mother of Saint Augustine of Hippo. Kessler's hotel collection has grown to include a dozen ultra-luxurious hotels and lodges across the country, including Beaver Creek Lodge in Colorado and El Monte Sagrado in Taos, New Mexico. The Kessler hotels then became part of the Marriot Autograph Collection of independent hotels when it formed in 2010.

Casa Monica resembles a palace as much as a hotel. The exquisite restoration included rebuilding the original hotel's carriage entrance. The elegant lobby features a bronze fountain, antique chandeliers, and

CASA MONICA HOTEL

historic maps and original Jean Claude Roy artwork on the walls. The rooms have Spanish wrought iron beds and mahogany furnishings. Each of the Casa Monica's five towers is a multistory luxury suite. During my stay in 2012, I found it to be both exceedingly elegant and ideally situated. I could easily walk to everything of interest in old St. Augustine.

Cordova 95, Casa Monica's renowned restaurant, serves fine dishes like coriander-crusted sea scallops and pan-seared duck with peach chutney. Café Cordova, the hotel's splendid coffee shop/bakery, opens onto a corner deck overlooking King Street and Flagler College.

Cedar House Inn
79 Cedar Street
St. Augustine 32084
(904) 829-0079
(800) 845-0012
www.cedarhouseinn.com

Carl Decker, a carpenter/builder who arrived in St. Augustine to take part in Henry Flagler's development boom, built this home in 1893 as his own and then built four others in the surrounding neighborhood on speculation. Over the years, Cedar House has been a private residence, a rental property, and, for a while in the 1970s, a fraternity house for Flagler College.

Russ and Nina Thomas bought the three-story Victorian in 1990 and converted it into a bed-and-breakfast in 1993 with just two rooms to rent. Today it has seven rooms. Cedar House Inn's current owner, Cyndi Humphrey, spent two decades in the hotel industry at the Ritz-Carlton and Four Seasons before purchasing the inn.

CEDAR HOUSE INN

Centennial House Bed & Breakfast
26 Cordova Street
St. Augustine 32084
(904) 810-2218
(800) 611-2880
www.centennialhouse.com

In 1997 Steve Bruyn and his family came across just what they were looking for in a bed-and-breakfast: a hundred-year-old, two-story frame house at the corner of Cordova and Saragossa Streets in the heart of St. Augustine's historic district. But the house was close to collapsing.

"The floor upstairs bounced so much we called it the trampoline," Steve explained to me when I met him in 2000. "The house had succumbed to a hundred years of rot, termites, and neglect. My guess

CENTENNIAL HOUSE BED & BREAKFAST

is that the owners must have lost everything in the crash of twenty-nine because by the early nineteen-thirties it had become a rooming house. And it deteriorated steadily from that point."

The family spent fourteen months rebuilding everything. Even the framing had to be replaced. They were able to recycle much of the disassembled materials, however. Four original chimneys, too fragile to leave standing, had to be taken down, but the antique bricks were reused to build a tropical courtyard beside the house. All sixty-four of the original window panes were removed and sent to a glass company to be reglazed. The Bruyns finished the restoration in 1999, and it looks as though it must have at the turn of the century but with the addition of all modern fixtures and accoutrements. The result is a warm and inviting inn with turn-of-the-century charm where everything works like new.

Centennial House has eight regally decorated rooms. The Fleur de Lis Room, downstairs in the main house, is fully ADA compliant and includes a roll-in shower and extra-wide doors. The inn sits two blocks from Flagler College along the horse carriage route, and the first-floor enclosed sunroom is the perfect place to relax and watch horses and carriages pass by. Behind the main house is Centennial's circa-1930s Carriage House. It was originally a garage with an upstairs apartment. The Bruyns removed the attic floor to give the house fourteen-foot-high cathedral ceilings.

Centennial House is now owned and operated by Lou and Beverly Stines.

INN ON CHARLOTTE STREET BED & BREAKFAST

Inn on Charlotte Street Bed & Breakfast
52 Charlotte Street
St. Augustine 32084
(904) 829-3819
(800) 355-5508
www.innoncharlotte.com

This two-story brick house was built in 1918 by attorney Levi Nelson, who later became St. Augustine's mayor. The large front porch, with wicker rocking chairs and a porch swing, invites guests to sit and read or sip tea. All eight rooms are decorated with period antiques. The carriage house is like a secret hideaway, tucked behind the main house. The Marjorie Rawlings Bungalow room sits downstairs, and Anna Marcotte's Hideaway is upstairs. I stayed in the upstairs hideaway prior to the inn's 2003 renovation. I found it charming then, and it is even more so today.

Kenwood Inn
38 Marine Street
St. Augustine 32084
(904) 824-2116
(800) 824-8151
www.thekenwoodinn.com

The Kenwood is a classic example of mid-nineteenth-century Victorian architecture, with a wide two-story veranda that wraps around three sides. Claw-foot bathtubs and four-poster beds, some with canopies, continue the Victorian theme in each room. The house was built in 1865 and opened as a boardinghouse in 1886, which might make it the oldest still-operating inn in St. Augustine. Located in the quiet southern end of the historic district, it is only a block west of the waterfront and a block north of St. Augustine's Oldest House. Owners Pat and Ted Dubosz both have experience in hotel and resort property management in south Florida, the Bahamas, and the Caribbean. In 2011 the inn's thirteen rooms underwent a renovation. Bathrooms were updated, and Jacuzzis were added to some rooms.

KENWOOD INN

Old Powder House Inn
38 Cordova Street
St. Augustine 32084
(800) 447-4149
www.oldpowderhouse.com

The house that is now the Old Powder House Inn was built in 1899 and sits on property where, a century before that, soldiers warehoused gunpowder during the second Spanish occupation of St. Augustine. Today the nine-room Powder House Inn is owned by Kal and Katie Kalieta. In contrast to the history of Old Powder House's location, the inn's rooms are decorated in bright Victorian florals. The Garden Suite has an adjoining sunroom with an additional bed.

OLD POWDER HOUSE INN

Saragossa Inn Bed & Breakfast
34 Saragossa Street
St. Augustine 32084
(904) 808-7384
(877) 808-7384
www.saragossainn.com

This 1924 Sears Craftsman bungalow in the quiet northwest residential section of the historic district was restored and converted into a bed-and-breakfast in 1990. Four of the six rooms have two beds, which makes the Saragossa well suited for families. The Homewood Room is a two-bedroom suite made from the original living room.

St. Francis Inn Bed & Breakfast
279 St. George Street
St. Augustine 32084
(904) 824-6068
(800) 824-6062
www.stfrancisinn.com

There is "old" in St. Augustine, and then there is "very old." The St. Francis Inn falls into the latter category. It was built in 1791 and is one of only a few true Spanish Colonial buildings left in Florida. While it has not functioned continuously as an inn, it is likely the oldest building that is currently an inn in St. Augustine.

Just eight years after Spain reacquired Florida from Great Britain, Spanish infantry Sergeant Gaspar Garcia built his home in St. Augustine on land granted to him by the king of Spain. It was not unusual for Spain to grant property to soldiers as a reward for meritorious duty. During those tumultuous times, homes were built to withstand attack. Garcia built his from thick coquina limestone—similar to the walls of nearby Fort Castillo de San Marcos—and he built it flush against the corner formed by what are now St. Francis and St. George Streets. The only problem was that those two streets did not cross at a precise right angle. To make it fit, Garcia built his house in a slightly trapezoidal shape. As a result, there are no perfectly square or rectangular rooms in the inn.

Current owners Joe and Margaret Finnegan purchased the St. Francis Inn in 1985 and in 1996 renovated its interior. The Finnegans have compiled a thorough chronology of prior owners of the house. Many were military figures, like British Marine Colonel Thomas Dummett, who purchased it in 1838. The colonel's daughter, Anna Dummett, was the first to convert the home to an inn. Anna's brother-in-law, Confederate Major William Hardee, purchased it in 1855 and then sold it to John Wilson in 1888. It was Wilson who added the

ST. FRANCIS INN BED & BREAKFAST

third floor and mansard roof to the main inn. He also built several surrounding buildings, one of which is the Wilson House across the street, which houses two suites for the St. Francis Inn. From 1894 on, the main house was variously rented as a residence and as apartments and also operated as a hotel. It was owner Ralph Moody who gave it the name St. Francis Inn in 1948.

Manager Mary Sparks took me on a tour of some of the notable rooms. Elizabeth's Room is a two-room suite with a large sitting room and a kitchenette cleverly built into a former closet. It overlooks St. Francis Park across the street. Anna's Room is smaller but has access to the balcony that sits above the inn's shaded courtyard and the St. Francis of Assisi statue and fountain. All of the first- and second-floor rooms have fireplaces. The inn was hosting a wedding party the day I visited, and they were taking pictures in the Balcony Room, the inn's premier room, with floor-to-ceiling windows, a two-person Jacuzzi, and its own private balcony.

Ghosts of St. Augustine (Pineapple Press) author Dave Lapham reports that the St. Francis Inn has a ghost. As legend tells it, Major Hardee's son and Lilly, a black slave, were madly in love, something that was strictly taboo in the nineteenth century. The young Hardee, distraught over his dilemma, committed suicide. But he's not the ghost. It is Lilly who has been seen walking the halls of the St. Francis Inn.

St. George Inn
4 St. George Street
St. Augustine 32084
(904) 827-5740
(888) 827-5740
www.stgeorge-inn.com

St. George Inn is tucked away at the north end of pedestrian St. George Street across from the historic City Gate. The inn has twenty-five spacious, comfortable rooms and suites and wraps around a

ST. GEORGE INN

cobblestone courtyard with shops and a great coffee shop, City Perks. I stayed in the large second-floor Santa Maria Room, which had terrific views of the City Gate and cemetery out of the side windows and of Fort Castillo de San Marcos out of the front windows.

Victorian House Bed & Breakfast
11 Cadiz Street
St. Augustine 32084
(904) 824-5214
(877) 703-0432
www.victorianhouse-inn.com

Victorian House sits in the quieter and older historic neighborhood south of King Street. It was built in 1897 by Alberto Rogero, whose ancestors were Minorcans who settled in St. Augustine a century earlier. There are five rooms in the main house, plus six suites in the adjacent carriage house. The current owners are Anthony and Marilyn Sexton.

Westcott House on the Bayfront
146 Avenida Menendez
St. Augustine 32084
(904) 825-4602
(800) 513-9814
www.westcotthouse.com

Dr. John Westcott arrived in St. Augustine in the 1850s and soon became involved in its development, particularly in transport. One of his projects, the St. Johns Railroad, ran tracks from the San Sebastian River, which runs right through St. Augustine, to the town of Tocoi to the west on the St. Johns River. He was also instrumental in promoting

VICTORIAN HOUSE BED & BREAKFAST

WESTCOTT HOUSE ON THE BAYFRONT

the Intracoastal Waterway, which runs through Matanzas Bay right in front of his house. The circa-1880 Westcott House's location at the south end of Avenida Menendez was obviously chosen to take advantage of the terrific views of Matanzas Bay.

Westcott House was restored and converted into a bed-and-breakfast in 1983. There are twelve rooms in the main house, plus four more in the carriage house. All sixteen rooms are furnished with turn-of-the-century antiques, and most have Jacuzzis (some double Jacuzzis) and electric fireplaces. The view of the bay from one of the big wicker chairs on the wraparound porches is unparalleled. Owners Andrew and Joy Warren spent many years in the hotel and hospitality industry in California before purchasing Westcott House in 2009.

St. Augustine Beach

BEACHFRONT BED & BREAKFAST

Beachfront Bed & Breakfast
1 F Street
St. Augustine Beach 32080
(904) 461-8727
(800) 370-6036
www.beachfrontbandb.com

This is something inexplicably rare in Florida: a bed-and-breakfast on the beach. The Beachfront has five rooms in the main beach house and three more rooms in the cottage behind it. The beach house, thought to have originally belonged to one of Henry Flagler's attorneys, was built in 1926 and converted to a bed-and-breakfast in 1999. Although the inn looks simple from the outside, dark wood paneling and floors give the interior of the main house an African safari lodge feel.

Amenities include a large swimming pool and something no old beach house in Florida is complete without: a shuffleboard court. Current owners Rich and Lauren O'Brien purchased Beachfront Bed & Breakfast in 2005.

CENTRAL WEST

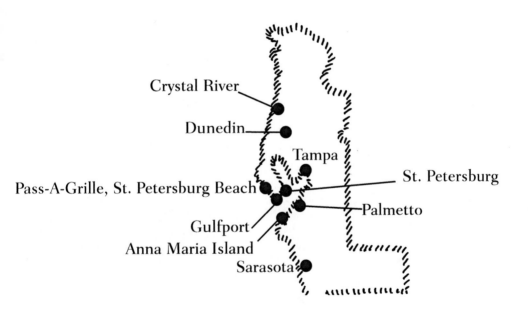

Crystal River

Dunedin

Tampa

Pass-A-Grille, St. Petersburg Beach

St. Petersburg

Palmetto

Gulfport

Anna Maria Island

Sarasota

CRYSTAL RIVER

Plantation Golf Resort and Spa
9301 West Fort Island Trail
Crystal River 34429
(352) 795-4211
(800) 632-6262
www.plantationinn.com

This expansive Southern-style plantation inn was built in 1962. It sits in the middle of 230 wildlife-preserve acres along the banks of Kings Bay, the headwaters of Crystal River, one of Florida's most popular destinations for freshwater scuba diving and swimming with manatees. The inn has its own dive shop, and the owners will arrange manatee swimming tours, kayaking, or tee times at their golf course.

PLANTATION GOLF RESORT AND SPA

DUNEDIN

The town of Dunedin dates back to the early 1870s, when Scottish immigrants John Ogilvie Douglas and James Somerville opened the Douglas and Somerville General Store. In 1878 Douglas and Somerville petitioned for an official United States post office in their store, and they submitted the name Dunedin. It's likely that the two abbreviated and combined their respective hometowns, Dundee and Edinburgh, and arrived at Dun-Edin.

The Orange Belt Railroad arrived in town in 1888, and by the turn of the century Dunedin had developed into a vital Gulf Coast rail depot in addition to a seaport for shipments of local citrus and cotton.

Dunedin has always been its own little town despite being an adjunct to Clearwater. So when word came that the Pinellas Trail would open up through downtown Dunedin in 1991, the town recognized a golden opportunity. What was once a nuisance—a defunct railroad crossing right in the middle of downtown—would become an attraction, drawing potential customers in the form of walkers, joggers, bicyclists, and rollerbladers into a waning district. Developers quickly went to work on plans to revitalize Main Street, with the Trail's crossing as its centerpiece. The result has been a resounding success. Downtown Dunedin is now a lively, pedestrian-friendly district with tree-lined brick walkways, restaurants, galleries, and shops, some of which front the Trail.

MERANOVA INN BED & BREAKFAST

Meranova Inn Bed & Breakfast
458 Virginia Lane
Dunedin 34698
(727) 733-9248
www.meranova.com

Only a block from the center of Dunedin, the Meranova sits on quiet, residential Virginia Lane. With a white picket fence out front and a gazebo in the side yard, the inn gives the feeling of visiting a friend's country home. Thoroughly renovated in 1999, the inn has seven rooms and suites in the main house, plus a charming cottage behind the house.

St. Pete Beach

Loews Don CeSar Hotel
3400 Gulf Boulevard
St. Petersburg Beach 33706
(727) 360-1881
(800) 282-1116
www.loewshotels.com/en/Don-CeSar-Hotel

The "Pink Palace," the "Pink Elephant," the "Wedding Cake." I knew the Don CeSar as the "Pink Monster" when I was growing in Tampa in the 1960s. It was a dilapidated, government-owned building that housed, among other things, a regional Veterans Administration office. When the government abandoned it in 1969, there wasn't much pink left. Afterward, it deteriorated into a hulking (and rumors said haunted) boarded-up castle. It had been an Army hospital in the early 1940s, with the entire eighth floor converted into operating rooms. Stories floated around that late at night you could still hear the screams of the ghosts of combat soldiers having limbs amputated without sufficient anesthesia.

It sat unattended for several years, subject to vandals, vagrants, and the elements. Eventually Pinellas County commissioners decided that they would put a park there if the federal government would just blow the old building up. That was when a group of local residents formed a "Save the Don" committee. Spurred on by newspaper articles written by June Hurley, they made it their mission to find a buyer who would restore the building. They found that buyer in St. Petersburg Beach Holiday Inn owner William Bowman Jr., who bought the old Don in 1972 for a reported $400,000.

The restoration was a monumental undertaking, the work tedious. Thirteen thousand panes of original glass had to be removed, scraped,

LOEWS DON CESAR HOTEL

and reinstalled. Bowman went to great lengths to be as historically accurate as possible, but he also needed to update the building with modern conveniences: central air-conditioning, new plumbing, and new electrical systems. The restored Don CeSar Hotel opened on November 24, 1973, although it took almost two more years to complete the entire restoration. The following year, the Don was added to the National Register of Historic Places.

The Don CeSar Hotel has become *the* symbol of St. Petersburg Beach. The ten-story, stucco Mediterranean Revival structure is clearly visible from the Sunshine Skyway Bridge ten miles south. Six towers with belfry arches rise from its red barrel-tile roofs. Red-and-white striped awnings shade balconies and penthouse terraces. A wide driveway that crosses over the top of Gulf Boulevard leads to the front entrance of the second-floor lobby. Inside, marble floors, arched entryways, soaring ceilings, chandeliers, and grand pianos lend an air of 1920s' opulence. You would feel right at home in a tuxedo, although most people walking through the lobby are wearing shorts and T-shirts over bathing suits. The beach side of the Don CeSar is a paradise with pools, tiki bars, palm trees, and bougainvillea vines. It all spills out onto the glistening white beach, lined with beach chairs.

Thomas J. Rowe was a Norfolk, Virginia, real estate broker who was in poor health and living from month to month when he moved to St. Petersburg in 1919, just in time for the land boom. Within six years, both his health and his financial situation had improved immensely. In 1925 he bought eighty acres, some of it beachfront, at the north end of Passe-A-Grille (south St. Pete Beach) from developer Perry Snell. Rowe's original plan called for a residential neighborhood of Spanish-style homes, but he also wanted a centerpiece: a grand hotel. To generate cash in order to build his hotel, he began subdividing the property and selling off lots.

Construction began on the hotel in 1925. Rowe hired contractor Carleton Beard and Indianapolis architect Henry DuPont. Halfway through construction, he fired DuPont because the hotel looked too plain. Rowe and Beard had been over to Boca Raton and Miami and admired the architecture of Addison Mizner and George Merrick. That's what they wanted. They decided that they could do without plans. They would design the rest of the hotel as they built it.

The Don CeSar opened with much fanfare on January 16, 1928. It was a huge success in its first twenty months of operation until October 29, 1929, when the stock market crashed. Occupancy dropped to a fraction of what it had been, and Rowe couldn't meet his mortgage obligations. The hotel went into receivership, but Rowe was still allowed to manage it. He worked night and day and, despite poor economic times, managed to build up business once again. At one point he signed the New York Yankees for a three-year contract of spring training seasons. For a while, Lou Gehrig, Babe Ruth, and other ball players were regular faces at the Don CeSar. Other famous (and infamous) guests included F. Scott Fitzgerald, Clarence Darrow, Franklin D. Roosevelt, and even Al Capone.

By the end of the 1930s, Thomas Rowe had paid off his debts and owned the hotel again. Then, in May 1940, he died. He had asked his lawyer to draw up a new will that would leave the hotel to his employees, but Rowe passed away before signing it. Mary Rowe, his estranged wife (they had been separated for decades), inherited the Don CeSar. She had never even set foot in it before. Mary appointed her attorney, Frank Harris, as president. One year later, World War II broke out and business plummeted again. Harris was negotiating a deal to lease the hotel to the United States Navy as officers' residences when, without warning, the U.S. government condemned the hotel and allowed the army to buy it for its paltry, tax-assessed value of $450,000. The government turned it into an army hospital and then converted it into an Air Force psychiatric/convalescent hospital in the 1940s. The Veteran's Administration moved in in 1945.

Today everyone knows the Don CeSar Hotel as simply the "Don." Don Caesar De Bazan (yes, the spelling is different), by the way, is a fictional hero in the Vincent Wallace opera *Maritana*. In an odd parallel to the hotel's own history, the character Don in *Maritana* is ordered by Spain's King Charles II to be executed by firing squad, but the guns misfire and he lives. Apparently Thomas Rowe was a fan of the opera— or at least a fan of a young Spanish opera singer named Lucinda, whom he had met in his younger years. Hotel staff sometimes report seeing a man who resembles photos of Thomas Rowe, walking the hotel grounds late at night with a beautiful, dark-haired Latin woman.

In 2003 the Don was purchased by Loews Hotels. Today it offers 277 rooms, including 36 suites, an 11,000-square-foot spa, 2 restaurants, 3 bars, and an ice cream parlor.

Pass-A-Grille

According to Allen Morris's *Florida Place Names* (Pineapple Press), maps dating back to 1841 identify Pass-A-Grille as "Passe-aux-Grilleurs," probably named for the fishermen who would stop on the beaches to smoke their day's catch in order to preserve it for the trip home. Civil War veteran Zephaniah Philips was the first to plat streets in Pass-A-Grille in 1890. Then in 1919, developer William McAdoo from North Carolina built the first bridge from the mainland to the island. That same year, as a publicity stunt, McAdoo buried a fake treasure chest in the sand on the next island north, which is where its name, Treasure Island, came from. A ferry out of Gulfport had been carrying visitors to Pass-A-Grille's beach since 1906, but it was not until McAdoo built his bridge that development began in earnest. Although Zephaniah Philips' family was the first to homestead there, Pass-A-Grille's original inhabitants were Tocobaga Indians who lived throughout the Tampa Bay area and built mounds on nearby Tierra Verde and at Safety Harbor.

Today Pass-A-Grille is a quiet beach town on the south end of St. Pete Beach, populated by as many pelicans as people. Well-preserved clapboard cottages hearken back to the 1920s, '30s, and '40s. Most of the town was designated a National Historic District in 1989 (with expanded designation in 2003), with more than three hundred buildings declared historic. One unique aspect of Pass-A-Grille is its mile-long public beach, fronted by Gulf Way Boulevard instead of houses. For most of its length, sea oat–covered dunes separate the beach from the road.

COCONUT INN

Coconut Inn
113 Eleventh Avenue
Pass-A-Grille 33706

Sabal Palms Inn
1301 Gulf Way
Pass-A-Grille 33706
(727) 367-3030
(800) 770-4853
www.coconutinnflorida.com

Coconut Inn has eleven studio and suite rooms half a block off the
beach, plus ten more at the newly acquired Sabal Palms Inn, a couple
of blocks down the road across from the beach.

Inn on the Beach
1401 Gulf Way
Pass-A-Grille 33706
(727) 360-8844
www.innonbeach.com

This quaint two-story inn right across from the beach is like a time capsule from the 1950s. There are twelve colorfully decorated rooms, some with their own balconies, plus four cottages with kitchens.

INN ON THE BEACH

Island's End Resort
1 Pass-A-Grille Way
Pass-A-Grille 33706
(727) 360-5023
www.islandsend.com

Island's End is a cluster of clapboard cottages at the southern tip of Pass-A-Grille, right on the Intracoastal Waterway. There are five one-bedroom cottages, all with kitchens, plus a waterfront three-bedroom cottage with its own pool. And Island's End has its own fishing dock.

ISLAND'S END RESORT

ST. PETERSBURG

Throughout the 1950s, '60s, and '70s, retirement haven St. Petersburg was known for the "world's largest shuffleboard complex"; its signature green park benches; Webb's City, the "world's most unusual drugstore"; and the *St. Petersburg Evening Independent* newspaper, which was free any day it rained. The 1990s saw an unprecedented downtown renaissance. With concerts and festivals at waterfront Straub Park, new museums, galleries, upscale shops, and fine restaurants, downtown St. Petersburg reinvented itself into a cultural and culinary destination that arguably makes it Florida's finest big-city downtown today. It's not just your grandparents' St. Petersburg anymore.

In 1881 Philadelphia saw manufacturer Hamilton Disston (with some help from investors) bought 6,000 square miles of southwest Florida swampland that also included 150,000 acres of not-so-swampy land on the Pinellas peninsula. It was a deal the State of Florida was more than happy to make at a time when the state's bankruptcy may have been just around the corner. Disston had proposed a city that would spread over many miles, but the town that was built on Boca Ciega Bay—alternately named Bonafacio, Disston City, Veteran City, and finally Gulfport—was considerably smaller. In 1886, in an effort to stay one step ahead of Henry Plant, Disston approached Russian immigrant and fledgling railroad owner Peter Demens. The year before, Demens, who owned a large sawmill outside of Orlando, was selling railroad ties to the failing Orange Belt Railroad. When Orange Belt could not pay its bills, Demens took over its charter and completed the line along the St. Johns River to Lake Apopka. Disston convinced Demens to extend that line across the state to Pinellas County. But Demens, who was quite short on funds himself, made it only as far as the eastern shore of Tampa Bay, well north of Disston's town. That's why St. Petersburg's downtown is where it is today instead of in Gulfport, where Disston had intended it. It was Demens who chose the name for this sunny new community at its terminus. Surely he recognized the irony when he named it after chilly St. Petersburg (Leningrad) in Russia.

Land on the north side of St. Petersburg was mostly citrus groves and swampy shoreline until Perry Snell came along. Snell was a Louisville, Kentucky, pharmacist when he married wealthy Tennessee heiress Lillian Allen in 1899. They honeymooned in St. Petersburg and loved it so much that, five years later, they returned there to live. Snell was convinced that St. Petersburg was going to grow. In 1906, financed with Lillian's inheritance, he started Bay Shore Development Company. He and partner J.C. Hamlett began buying property north of downtown, some from the Orange Belt Railroad's St. Petersburg Land Improvement Company, some from the Tison-Turner Company of Savannah, Georgia, and some grove acreage from Chicagoan Erastus Barnard. By 1910 they owned most of the land along the south side of Coffee Pot Bayou and down the northeast shore of Tampa Bay, halfway to downtown. In 1911 home construction had begun in earnest, but Snell understood that there was more to building a neighborhood than just drawing streets and selling lots. It required infrastructure. So he dredged and filled the low land, built a seawall around Coffee Pot Bayou, and paid out of his own pocket for the extension of the city's trolley line up to Coffee Pot Bayou. Then, in a move that many must have thought was pure foolishness, he donated the most valuable section of his property–along the Tampa Bay shoreline–to the city with the agreement that St. Petersburg officials would turn it into a waterfront park. Today North Shore Park is a place where people picnic, jog, walk their dogs, and toss Frisbees. It adds immeasurably to the value of the neighborhood and the rest of downtown St. Petersburg.

Snell's Old Northeast is the oldest platted neighborhood in St. Petersburg. It was placed on the National Register of Historic Places in 2003. At 425 acres, it is one of the largest designated historic districts in Florida.

DICKENS HOUSE BED & BREAKFAST

Dickens House Bed & Breakfast
335 Eighth Avenue Northeast
St. Petersburg 33701
(727) 822-8622
(800) 381-2022
www.dickenshouse.com

St. Petersburg's historic Old Northeast neighborhood has some of this area's finest examples of Arts and Crafts homes, sometimes called bungalow or Craftsman style. One of the best is the authentically renovated 1912 Henry and Sadie Dickens House, now the Dickens House Bed & Breakfast. In 1995 Rhode Island School of Design graduate and artist Ed Caldwell purchased and restored the house. Ed spent four years on the restoration, and his design expertise shows. He has turned the house into one of the most striking examples of Arts and Crafts architecture in a bed-and-breakfast I have seen.

Renaissance Vinoy Resort and Golf Club
501 Fifth Avenue NE
St. Petersburg 33701
(727) 894-1000
(888) 303-4430
www.vinoyrenaissanceresort.com

The Vinoy connects the north end of downtown St. Petersburg with the south end of the historic Old Northeast neighborhood and overlooks the Vinoy Marina and the Million Dollar pier on Tampa Bay. In 1923 Pennsylvania oil tycoon Aymer Vinoy Laughner bought property next door to his St. Petersburg home and hired New York architect Henry Taylor to design what would become a $3.5-million Spanish-Mediterranean palace. It took only ten months to construct, and when it opened on New Year's Eve 1925, it was the town's most luxurious hotel and the perfect upscale anchor for flourishing downtown St. Petersburg.

Even through the collapse of the Florida land boom and subsequent Depression, the Vinoy maintained its elegant ambience and continued to attract notable clientele like Calvin Coolidge, Herbert Hoover, F. Scott Fitzgerald, and Babe Ruth. During World War II, Laughner leased the hotel to the Army Air Corps as a training headquarters. Shortly after, he sold it to Charles Alberding's Alsonett Hotels, which also owned downtown St. Petersburg's Soreno Hotel. Alberding upheld the Vinoy's tradition of grandeur well into the 1950s, but overwhelming maintenance on the aging structure and a lack of air-conditioning took their toll in the 1960s. By the early 1970s, the building had declined into a low-rent boardinghouse (reportedly $7 a night). Finally, in 1974, it closed down.

RENAISSANCE VINOY RESORT AND GOLF CLUB

The once-grand Vinoy sat boarded up and deteriorating for sixteen years. Then it was saved from the wrecking ball when Stouffer Hotels and Frederick Guest's Vinoy Development Company bought it in 1990. Two years and $93 million later, it reopened as the Stouffer Vinoy. Restorers were able to save much of the original detail work, including hand-stenciled pecky cypress ceiling beams and Pompeii-themed frescoes. In a repeat of its earliest history, the Vinoy once again set the tone and character for a booming downtown St. Petersburg.

Renaissance Hotels and Resorts, a division of Marriot Hotels, bought Stouffer Hotels in 1993 and changed the Vinoy's name to Renaissance Vinoy Resort in 1996. Renaissance still owns and operates the Vinoy. Between the original main hotel and the newer tower building next to it, the Vinoy has 361 rooms and suites. All are quite spacious, including those in the original hotel, thanks to the renovators expanding every one and a half original rooms into single larger rooms and baths. I stayed in one of the tower rooms with a balcony overlooking the tennis courts and St. Petersburg's historic Old Northeast neighborhood beyond.

Since its renovation, the Vinoy has had regular updates and additions to keep it fresh and new for returning guests. In 2012 a newly renovated lobby became an inviting gathering space. One of the most interesting changes is a new library across from the lobby bar. It opens onto the promenade but is a distinct and comfortable personal space with wormwood paneling and bookcases accented by bright abstract rugs. The abstract rug theme cleverly continues onto the main lobby's floor, adding a dash of Art Deco without compromising the Vinoy's historic ambience. The Vinoy has six restaurants, ranging from elegant (Marchand's and Fred's Steakhouse) to the casual-tropical (Alfresco's). I feasted on lobster hash with poached eggs and French toast with banana glaze sauce at the Sunday brunch at Marchand's.

GULFPORT

Peninsula Inn and Spa
2937 Beach Boulevard
Gulfport 33707
(727) 346-9800
(888) 900-0466
www.innspa.net

For fifteen years, whenever I visited Gulfport, the question would always come up: "When is someone going to do something with that old clapboard hotel in the middle of town?" Occasionally it would

PENINSULA INN AND SPA

open up temporarily for special events, but the inn had been closed since 1985. It was called the Suncoast Inn back then, but it was the Bayview Hotel when it first opened in 1905, when there still may have been a glimmer of hope that Gulfport (Disston City then) would become a thriving metropolis. In 1999 Jim and Alexandra Kingzett bought the property and began the intensive task of bringing the old hotel back to life. Finally, in 2002, after completely renovating the interior and rebuilding much of the exterior, the couple opened the Peninsula Inn. Today the inn has eleven rooms and suites, a spa, and two restaurants: Isabelle's, which serves Southern low-country cuisine, and Six Tables at Peninsula. Furnishings from Indonesia give the lobby and rooms just a hint of Bali Hai. The Kingzetts have done a fine job of both maintaining the inn's historic character and making it an inviting place to stay.

Sea Breeze Manor Bed & Breakfast
5701 Shore Blvd
Gulfport 33707
(727) 343-4445
(888) 343-4445
www.seabreezemanor.com

Local Gulfport residents used to call Sea Breeze Manor the Storm House because, with its twelve-inch-thick walls, it was the safest place to seek sanctuary during a hurricane. Built in 1923, it remained a private residence until Patty and Lawrence Burke purchased it in 1996 and opened the Sea Breeze Manor. The Burkes were construction contractors before getting into the bed-and-breakfast business. By the looks of their renovation of the Sea Breeze, they must have been very good contractors. The restoration and remodeling are exceptional. Every detail, inside and out, is perfect.

The Sea Breeze Manor fits perfectly in quaint, colorful Gulfport, a tranquil arts community on the shores of Boca Ciega Bay. Tiny Gulfport is self-contained but encapsulated within the big city of St. Petersburg. Galleries, antiques stores, arts-and-crafts shops, and restaurants line Beach Boulevard for half a dozen blocks. At the bay, turn west on Shore Boulevard, drive four blocks, and the Sea Breeze Manor is on the right.

Painted sea green with white trim and a bright red roof, the house combines Tudor architecture with a dash of the Caribbean, thanks to tropical landscaping, green-and-white striped umbrellas, and Bahamian shutters. There are four suites in the main house, plus an attached cottage on the west side of the house and a detached cottage

SEA BREEZE MANOR BED & BREAKFAST

on the northwest side (once a schoolhouse the original owners built for their disabled child). A lush garden courtyard separates the cottage from the house.

Each room is named for an exotic tropical location. I've stayed in the Jamaica Suite on the second floor twice. Colorful paintings of tropical scenes hang on the walls. French doors open onto a private wraparound balcony with Adirondack chairs, a perfect place to spend the morning watching pelicans soar over the bay. The bathroom is enormous—ten by twelve feet—and has a stand-up shower and a separate tub with its own window.

Lori Rosso had spent two decades working out of Washington, D.C., organizing tour delegations and advance arrangements for executives, dignitaries, and, ultimately, President George H.W. Bush. In 2002 she purchased the Sea Breeze Manor from the Burkes. Lori has put her extensive hospitality expertise to fine use here, offering guests a perfect place to escape from the pressures of daily life.

TAMPA

Florida had been a United States territory for three years when U.S. Infantry Colonel George Brooke established a fort in 1824 at the mouth of the Hillsborough River in what is now downtown Tampa. Brooke's troops, however, were not the first outsiders to settle here. Since the 1790s, Spanish and Cuban fishermen had been living in a small thatched-hut village called Spanishtown along a creek just across the river. But Tampa's real development as a city began with the arrival of railroad mogul Henry B. Plant in 1881. See A Tale of Two Henrys, which follows my Introduction, to read a detailed account of Henry Plant's life.

Don Vicente de Ybor Historic Inn
1915 Republica de Cuba/14th Street
Tampa 33605
(813) 241-4545
(866) 206-4545
www.donvicenteinn.com

Ybor City, east Tampa's historic cigar factory district, was settled and populated by Spanish, Cuban, and Italian immigrants who arrived to work in the cigar industry. Spaniard Vicente Martinez Ybor was a tobacco merchant from Cuba who opened the first cigar factory in Tampa in 1886 and developed the community that would become Ybor City. Within two decades, Ybor City had become the cigar capital of the world.

In 2000 historic renovator and Tampa native Jack Shiver put the finishing touches on his Don Vicente de Ybor Historic Inn in the two-story structure that was known for more than half a century as the Gonzalez Medical Clinic. It was originally constructed in 1895 as an office building, pharmacy, and café and then converted into a mutual-

Don Vicente de Ybor Historic Inn

aid clinic for cigar factory workers in 1903. Dr. Aurelio Gonzalez purchased the clinic in 1937, and the building served in that capacity for forty years before closing. Shiver bought the property in 1998 and began a $2-million renovation. This was not Shiver's first restoration: He's done eleven other Ybor City buildings. His first was the Gutierrez Building on Seventh Avenue, Ybor's main street.

The Don Vicente de Ybor is a sixteen-room inn with two suites, one with a king-size Murphy bed to easily convert it into a hospitality room. The lobby is richly appointed in wood and brass with a grand marble staircase. The inn also has an elegant dining room, an underground "speakeasy" lounge, and a café that features a restored carved wooden bar that came from Tampa's old Sea Wolf Restaurant.

Floridan Palace Hotel
905 North Florida Avenue
Tampa 33602
(813) 225-1700
www.floridanpalace.com

Until the twenty-two-story Exchange Bank building went up in 1966, the Floridan Hotel was downtown Tampa's tallest building: nineteen floors topped with a giant red sign that lit up the skyline at night. In fact, when it opened in 1927, the Floridan was the tallest skyscraper in all of Florida.

Allen Simms was a classic self-made man. He had left home as a teenager to become a lumberjack in Canada. A decade later, he showed up in Tampa and began acquiring and developing real estate. The 1920s was a golden age of expansion in Florida—Tampa's population actually doubled in that decade—and Simms rode that wave to become one of Tampa's most prolific developers. In 1925 he planned the construction of a high-rise luxury hotel in downtown Tampa. For its design, he hired prominent architect Francis J. Kennard, the same

FLORIDAN PALACE HOTEL

architect Henry Plant had hired to design his 1897 Belleview Biltmore Hotel in Clearwater.

It took just one year to complete, opening on January 15, 1927. The steel-frame, brick-and-granite building's reported construction cost was $2 million—plus an additional $1 million to furnish and decorate—an exorbitant amount for that time. But this was a lavish hotel and the tallest in the state in an era when prosperity seemed endless. No expense was spared in its embellishment: crystal chandeliers, marble floors, luxurious furniture and rugs. But within three years, the Florida boom would come to a resounding crash. Simms had no choice but to sell the hotel. Baron Collier's Collier Florida Hotels Company purchased it. Collier, one of the largest landowners in Florida, had the finances to weather the economic collapse, and so the Floridan survived through the 1930s. During World War II, the Floridan became a busy place again. Of particular note, the hotel's Sapphire Room became a popular nightspot for servicemen stationed at MacDill Field and Drew Airfield. They called it the "Surefire Room."

Ownership shifted again in 1943 when a group of investors, the Florida Hotel Operating Company, bought into the Floridan. Through the years, the hotel hosted celebrities and dignitaries: Gary Cooper, Lupe Velez, Clarence Darrow, Babe Ruth, and Charlton Heston. Even Elvis Presley stayed at the Floridan in 1955 following a concert at Tampa's Fort Homer Hesterly Armory. But by the mid-1960s, the Floridan had lost much of its luster. Various owners from 1966 on tried to revitalize it, but none succeeded. For a few years in the early 1970s, it was a college dormitory for Patricia Stevens Career College. Mostly it was a flophouse (reportedly $14 a night in the 1980s). One bright spot came in 1996, when owner Akio Ogawa of Sity International Corporation obtained National Registry of Historic Places status for the hotel in an attempt to cinch a sale to Grand Heritage Hotels. The Grand Heritage deal fell through at the last minute, and the hotel finally sold to Capital LLC in 1997. In 2001 the Floridan was officially condemned. Capital patched it up just enough to keep the wrecking crews at bay. Then, in 2005, another buyer came along. Most people thought he would probably be just another in a long succession of unsuccessful owners, but they were wrong.

Antonio Markopoulos, who moved from his native Greece to Canada in the 1950s and later to the United States, owned a Days Inn hotel along with three other properties on Clearwater Beach. He had been working on a project to build a large beachfront resort there, but waiting for city approval had slowed progress, and Markopoulos decided to sell his properties for a reported $40 million. In 2005 he found a new project in the Floridan Hotel, which he bought for $6 million. This time the difference was that no financing was needed—Markopoulos could pay for the entire project out of his own pocket—and that he put his son Angelo in charge of running the hotel. No one will divulge how much was spent to restore the now-named Floridan Palace Hotel, but speculation has it in the $20 million range, and it certainly looks like it. Swarovski chandeliers hang from the lobby ceiling, whose floral medallion pattern took a team of artists and craftsmen a solid year to restore. The meticulous restoration required a level of craftsmanship that most thought was a long-lost art. From brass fixtures, marble flooring, and intricate cypress woodwork, to the re-creation of the Sapphire Room, to the elegant Crystal Dining Room, Markopoulos has accomplished what no one thought possible: the rebirth of the Floridan Hotel.

Markopoulos found the original, electric rooftop sign stored away in one of the upper rooms. It took two years to restore it, and in 2008 the sign lit up atop the Floridan for the first time in decades. Originally the Floridan had more than four hundred rooms. Back then, hotel rooms were typically much smaller than they are now, so Markopoulos doubled the size of the rooms. The hotel now has 195 rooms, plus 15 executive suites and 3 penthouse suites. The new Floridan Palace Hotel opened in 2012 and may be even more opulent than when it opened originally in 1927.

PALMETTO

Palmetto Riverside Bed and Breakfast
1102 Riverside Drive
Palmetto 34221
(941) 981-5331
www.palmettoriverside.com

Wim and Mieke Lippens moved from their native Belgium to Florida in the 1990s. After looking for several years, they found a 1913 Sears and Roebuck catalog home overlooking the Manatee River in Palmetto. Sears began offering homes in its catalog in 1908. You could have both the full plans and the pre-cut components of the house delivered directly to your lot. Over the next thirty years, Sears sold more than seven hundred thousand homes. This house had belonged to Julius and Lillie Lamb. Julius, son of Samuel Sparks Lamb, founder of the town of Palmetto, owned a horse stable and a dry goods store and eventually became a real estate broker and banker. This was the Lambs' second house. Their first house, built in 1899, is just around the corner.

The six-room Palmetto Riverside Bed and Breakfast has been immaculately restored, and the expansive, lushly landscaped grounds are a perfect setting for weddings and receptions, something the Lippenses specialize in.

PALMETTO RIVERSIDE BED AND BREAKFAST

ANNA MARIA, HOLMES BEACH, BRADENTON BEACH, ANNA MARIA ISLAND

Most assume that the name Anna Maria is of Spanish origin, and that's a reasonable assumption since Spanish explorers, including Ponce de Leon and Hernando de Soto, sailed this coast in the early 1500s (and Ponce de Leon did have a daughter named Maria). Old Spanish maps even show the island as Ana Maria Cay. Another contingent, however, claims that the name is Scottish and should be pronounced Anna Mar-EYE-a. Most of the island's longtime residents pronounce it with the long I.

George Emerson Bean stopped on uninhabited Anna Maria Island just south of the inlet to Tampa Bay sometime in the early

1890s while sailing from his home in Connecticut down to the Gulf. He fell in love with it and vowed to return with his family. In 1893 he filed for homestead on 160 acres on the north end of the island. Shortly thereafter, he and his sons built their family home there. Bean died in 1898, but his sons and their families continued to live and build on Anna Maria.

Charles John Roser was the baker who invented the recipe for Fig Newtons. He had just sold his recipe to Nabisco and moved to St. Petersburg to retire when he met George Bean Jr. In 1911 they teamed up to form the Anna Maria Beach Company and began the first commercial development of the island.

Anna Maria is one the few Florida beach towns that has retained its 1950s'–'60s' flavor. A local ordinance prohibits the construction of any building taller than three stories, preventing the invasion of high-rise condos.

ANNA MARIA BEACH COTTAGES

Anna Maria Beach Cottages
112 Oak Avenue
Anna Maria 34217
(941) 778-1503
(800) 778-2030
www.annamariabeachcottages.com

Anna Maria Beach Cottages is a collection of restored clapboard cottages and duplexes with a total of eleven suites, all with kitchens, just steps from the beach. There's a swimming pool as well. I stayed in the smallest cottage, 110B, and found it charming, brightly decorated, and very comfortable. It even has its own outdoor shower.

Bungalow Beach Resort
2000 Gulf Drive
North Bradenton Beach 34217
(800) 779-3601
www.bungalowbeach.com

BUNGALOW BEACH RESORT

Just south of Anna Maria, on Bradenton Beach, Bungalow Beach Resort is a collection of nicely restored (most from the 1930s) duplexes and quadruplexes on the beach side of Gulf Drive, plus a house just across the road. I stayed in the one-bedroom Coquina Bungalow. It has a vaulted ceiling with a skylight over the queen-size bed, a galley kitchen, and a tiny beachfront porch. The interior is decorated in comfortable *Coastal Living* style.

Harrington House Beachfront Bed & Breakfast
5626 Gulf Drive
Holmes Beach 34217
(941) 778-5444
(888) 828-5566
www.harringtonhouse.com

This large coquina, three-story house was built as a residence in 1925 and was once the home of Max Ingham, mayor of Holmes Beach in the 1950s. Frank and Jo Adele Davis bought and remodeled it in 1988 and opened Harrington House in 1989. Harrington was Frank Davis's father's name. The main house has seven rooms—two downstairs and five upstairs with Gulf-view balconies—plus a cottage immediately adjacent to it. In subsequent years, the Davises have expanded their property to include three more houses, four bungalows, a three-unit villa, and a condominium, giving Harrington House a total of twenty-eight accommodations.

I stayed in the one-room cottage right next to the main house. It has a queen-size bed, a heart-shaped Jacuzzi, and its own deck facing the beach. A gazebo sits in the shade of Australian pines just outside the door, and the Harrington House pool is just a couple of steps beyond that. All of the amenities that a beach house could have are available for guests: sea kayaks, beach-cruiser bikes, and a lobby bookcase filled with paperbacks.

There are no seawalls in front of the Harrington House. Sea oats, pine trees, and a favorable tide, which swirls around Anna Maria's Bean Point, fortify the wide, sandy beach.

SARASOTA

A great deal of Sarasota's early history centers around one person, John Ringling, best known as the man who brought the circus to town. But his interests and, ultimately, his influence in Sarasota extended beyond the big top. One of five brothers who started a circus business in 1884, John was initially in charge of transport. Within a few years, he had converted the show from wagons to railroads, greatly expanding its reach and propelling the circus's growth. In 1906 and 1907, Ringling Brothers bought out two competitors, including Barnum & Bailey.

In 1911 John and his wife, Mable, bought beach property in Sarasota for a summer home. With Florida's popularity on the rise, Ringling saw Sarasota's great potential as a summer resort town. In 1922 and 1923, he purchased a string of barrier islands, including St. Armands Key, Lido Key, Bird Key, and the south end of Longboat Key, intent on developing a resort community, Ringling Isles. Then in 1924, he built the bridge from downtown Sarasota to St. Armands Key. The following year, he and Mable constructed their colossal thirty-two-room Venetian Gothic home on Sarasota Bay, which they named Cà d'Zan, or "House of John" in the Venetian dialect.

In 1926 Florida land values began to nose-dive, and Ringling decided to move the entire Ringling Brothers and Barnum & Bailey Circus from Bridgeport, Connecticut, to Sarasota in an effort to revitalize the local economy. It paid off. Sarasota weathered the late 1920s better than the rest of Florida.

While the circus, the railroad, and property development were Ringling's professional pursuits, collecting art was his passion. John and Mable were frequent travelers to Europe and were particularly fond of Italy. They collected a considerable amount of art and furnishings from abroad. In 1927, on the grounds of Cà d'Zan, they established the John and Mable Ringling Museum of Art, but it was not completed until 1929—sadly, the year Mable died.

With the Florida land boom crash followed by the 1929 stock market crash and Mable's death that same year, John Ringling had suffered a barrage of personal and financial blows. He died in 1936, almost completely drained of his fortune. He left, however, an indelible mark on Sarasota. He was the town's foremost developer and its most ardent advocate, who almost single-handedly set the tone for the cultural atmosphere that Sarasota is known for today. In the end, of all he accumulated and lost, it was his passionate pursuit of art that retained the most value. Today the Ringling Museum of Art houses the Ringlings' collection of more than six hundred paintings, many sixteenth- and seventeenth-century Italian and Flemish Baroque, including an outstanding selection of Peter Paul Rubens, one of John Ringling's favorites.

Cypress Bed & Breakfast Inn
621 Gulfstream Avenue South
Sarasota 34236
(941) 955-4683
www.cypressbb.com

New Jersey natives Nina and Robert Belott and Vicki Hadley had decided to open a bed-and-breakfast in 1996 when they found this 1939 home across from Sarasota Bayfront Park. It features five rooms, three of which are spacious suites. The Martha Rose Suite has French doors opening onto a balcony overlooking the park and the bay.

CYPRESS BED & BREAKFAST INN

La Palme Royale Bed & Breakfast
624 South Palm Avenue
Sarasota 34236
(866) 800-3921
www.lprsrq.com

La Palme Royale offers four suites in this 1924 house.

CENTRAL

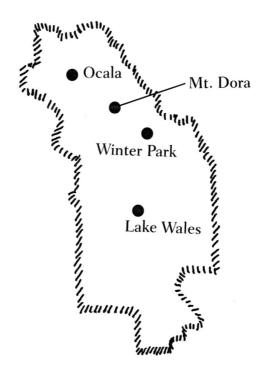

Ocala

Mt. Dora

Winter Park

Lake Wales

OCALA

This is horse country: rolling hills and pastures lined with endless white picket fences. Some of the fastest and most famous (and most expensive) racehorses in the world are bred in the farms that surround Ocala.

Seven Sisters Inn
828 East Fort King Street
Ocala 34471
(352) 433-0700
www.sevensistersinn.org

Norma and Jerry Johnson began restoring the circa-1888 Gordon Scott House in Ocala's historic Fort King Street district in 1985 and opened it as the Seven Sisters Inn the following year. They named the rooms after Norma's siblings, hence Seven Sisters.

In 1991 former commercial pilots Bonnie Morehardt and Ken Oden purchased Seven Sisters Inn and added the circa-1890 Rheinauer House next door, where Ocala mayor and prominent businessman Charles Rheinauer and his wife, Emma, lived from 1895 to 1925. But in 2009, the downturning economy took its toll, and both houses that comprised the inn were sold in foreclosure auction. Attorneys Richard Perry and Jim Richard purchased the properties and opened their law office in the Scott House. In 2012 the Historic Ocala Preservation Society moved its offices to the Scott House as well.

In 2010 Bob and Maria Schmidt purchased the Rheinhauer House from Perry and Richard. They spent two years remodeling and decorating and reopened once again as the Seven Sisters Inn. Each of the inn's five suites reflects an exotic international locale. The French antique–decorated Paris Suite had been the Rheinhauers' master bedroom. The Beijing Suite is decorated with Oriental antiques. King

SEVEN SISTERS INN

Tut watches over you in the Egyptian-themed Cairo Suite. The Madrid Suite has a four-poster canopy bed and an authentic 1940s' Spanish prison fireplace. The Casablanca Suite is decorated in a Moroccan palace style.

MOUNT DORA

Mount Dora is a storybook, picturesque town with tree-lined streets, Victorian street lamps, and a multitude of parks, antiques shops, galleries, and restaurants. The "mount" is really a bluff that sits above Lake Dora. This little town bustles with activity. The list of festivals and events is lengthy: an antique boat show in March, an antique automobile tour in April, an annual art festival in February, and bicycle

ADORA INN BED & BREAKFAST

festivals in October and March. The entire month of December is one long Christmas festival with a lighted boat parade, street parades, and elaborate decorations and lighting throughout the town.

Adora Inn Bed & Breakfast
610 North Tremain Street
Mount Dora 32757
(352) 735-3110
www.adorainn.com

The Adora Inn Bed & Breakfast, two blocks from Mount Dora's quaint downtown, is a beautifully restored three-story 1916 bungalow. Owners/innkeepers John Cataldo and Arthur Natale thoroughly renovated the house and have artfully applied a blend of mid-century modern style with traditional Arts and Crafts to the interior. The Adora is a charming, neighborhood, five-room bed-and-breakfast with gracious hosts and great food. Both John and Arthur have professional culinary backgrounds so you can expect gourmet breakfasts (and sometimes dinner on request). Although the inn has five rooms, there is a sixth option: The Camel Room can be expanded as a two-bedroom suite. My favorites are the upstairs Treehouse and Vanilla Rooms, with king-size beds that sit in the wide, third-floor, six-window dormer.

Lakeside Inn
100 North Alexander Street
Mount Dora 32757
(352) 383-4101
(800) 556-5016
www.lakeside-inn.com

Mount Dora's oldest standing structure, the Lakeside Inn, was built in 1883. Originally a ten-room hotel named the Alexander House, it was the joint project of key Mount Dora developers James Alexander, John MacDonald, and J.P. Donnelly. When they sold it in 1893, the name changed to Lake House. When it changed hands again in 1933, it became the Lakeside Inn. During the 1920s and '30s, the inn was the place to be in Mount Dora. One historic highlight of note: In the winter of 1930, former President and Mrs. Calvin Coolidge arrived at the inn for an extended sabbatical following Calvin's just-completed term as president. During their stay, Calvin dedicated the newly completed Gables and Terrace wings.

James Barggren and Richard Dempsey bought the Lakeside Inn in 1992 and meticulously restored it to its 1920s'–'30s' heyday style. Today the inn has eighty-five rooms and suites. I stayed in a second-floor room decorated in a 1930s' style in the Gables wing, overlooking the Olympic-size pool and the grass courtyard that slopes down to Lake Dora. With tennis courts and a boat-and-seaplane dock on the

LAKESIDE INN

lake, you'll never run out of activities. (The inn arranges sightseeing tours in a DeHavilland Beaver seaplane.) Perhaps the most enjoyable activity, though, is sitting in one of the rocking chairs on the main lodge's expansive veranda, sipping iced tea and soaking up the view across placid Lake Dora.

WINTER PARK

Bordering the northeast edge of the sprawling metropolis of Orlando is a picture-perfect oasis, a small town with winding brick streets, tree-lined sidewalks, tranquil parks, and an exceptional main street shopping district. It is also home to Rollins College, Florida's oldest college, established in 1885.

In 1881 Massachusetts developers Loring Chase and Oliver Chapman purchased six hundred acres near the small settlement of Osceola, intent on building a winter resort town. With the hope of attracting other New Englanders from their harsh winters, they named it Winter Park. The town was platted with parks and streets that wound around half a dozen lakes. The following year, a railroad depot opened and businesses began to sprout. One, the Seminole Hotel, was among Florida's most luxurious lodgings when it opened in 1886. Ironically, it was a hard freeze in 1895 that struck an economic blow to Winter Park and left Chase and Chapman in a financial bind. Chicago machinery manufacturing mogul Charles Hosmer Morse stepped in and purchased the assets of Chase and Chapman's Winter Park Company. Morse retired in Winter Park nine years later. He is credited with saving the town and, in the years that followed, contributing much to what it is today. Winter Park is aptly named, containing more than seventy parks. Most prominent is the eleven-acre Central Park, one of Morse's contributions, along the west side of Park Avenue.

Park Plaza Hotel
307 South Park Avenue
Winter Park 32789
(407) 647-1072
www.parkplazahotel.com

Park Avenue is Winter Park's bustling main street, with a beautiful tree-filled park on one side and fine shops, boutiques, galleries, and restaurants on the other. At its south end sits the Park Plaza Hotel, an elegant boutique hotel overlooking the avenue. It was originally named the Hamilton Hotel when it was built in 1922 by architect Peter Samwell. After John and Cissie Spang purchased it in 1977, the hotel underwent significant renovations. Today, rich mahogany

PARK PLAZA HOTEL

paneling and brass fixtures give the lobby intimate warmth. Twenty-eight rooms and suites are furnished with cushioned wicker chairs and brass beds. French doors open onto balconies with potted plants and hanging ferns. The Park Plaza Gardens restaurant is known for its Sunday brunch.

LAKE WALES

Chalet Suzanne
3800 Chalet Suzanne Drive
Lake Wales 33859
(863) 676-6011
(800) 433-6011
www.chaletsuzanne.com

Carl and Bertha Hinshaw had plans to develop a golf community in the rolling countryside near Lake Wales in the 1920s. Kraft Cheese Company president, J.L. Kraft, was to be a major partner, but the timing worked against them. The collapse of the Florida real estate market and the stock market crash of 1929 brought the project to a grinding halt. Then in 1931, Carl passed away from severe pneumonia at only forty-seven years of age. Bertha, left with two young children, Carl Jr. and Suzanne, was determined to find a way to provide for her family. That same year she opened Suzanne's Tavern (named for her daughter). Soon she changed the name to Suzanne's Chalet, and then later switched it around to Chalet Suzanne.

Duncan Hines (yes, the cake-baking Duncan Hines), an early patron, helped put Chalet Suzanne on the map when he included it in his book *Adventures in Good Eating*. (The first of many editions came out in the 1930s.)

CHALET SUZANNE

In the 1940s, a fire leveled the chalet. Upon returning from World War II, Carl Jr., along with Bertha, rebuilt it using whatever materials and resources he had at his disposal. Mother and son relocated several buildings, including part of a horse stable and a chicken house, to construct what would evolve into today's dining hall, which overlooks Lake Suzanne.

Today the Hinshaw Family continues to operate the storybook-like Chalet Suzanne, and it remains one of Florida's most enchanting and romantic places to stay and to dine. It is unlike any inn I've ever visited before, more like a Swiss village than an inn. You might think you've stepped into a fairy tale. The grounds spread across seventy acres. Rambling brick walkways meander past fountains, gardens, and courtyards and wind through the colorful village where each of the rooms (no two are alike) has its own entrance. A tiny antiques shop/museum and a ceramics shop are nestled at the east end.

The room I stayed in, Governor South, sits above the dining hall and shares a wraparound patio with Governor North on the dining hall roof. From the patio I had a sweeping view of the lake. Like a scene from an old Disney animated feature, turtles swam near the shore, herons wandered along the banks, and a huge black swan paddled leisurely across the water. Beyond the lake I could see one end of Chalet Suzanne's own lighted, 2,500-foot grass airstrip. Private pilots from around the state have been flying to Chalet Suzanne for dinner for many years.

The Governor South room itself is like a grotto. The plaster walls and ceiling are done in varying shades of peach and pink and seem almost free formed. At its entryway the ceiling is only about six feet high and then rises to the center of the room. Likewise, the floor cants uphill from one side. It reminds me of a fun house, where the slanting floor and ceiling give the illusion that a person is taller in one end of the room than in the other. It is furnished with European antiques: a writing desk, dresser, and bedside tables. A king-size round bed completes the nothing-is-square theme. If the White Rabbit and the Mad Hatter had popped out of the closet, I don't think I would have been completely surprised.

The night's stay includes breakfast, which is served from 8:00 until 11:00 A.M. There are no seating times. Just wander down whenever you like, which is nice, since that giant round bed and its twenty-two (I counted) pillows of various sizes and shapes conspire to want to make you sleep in. I had a choice of eggs Benedict or scrambled eggs and ham steak with delicious, sweet Swedish pancakes (like miniature crepes) topped with Swedish lingonberry jam, plus sticky cinnamon buns.

Dinner at Chalet Suzanne (not included in your stay except with special packages) is a six-course, all-evening affair that is quite elegant—and quite expensive. Entrees include king crab thermidor, Maine lobster Newburg, filet mignon, and crab sassé. Chalet Suzanne's gourmet meals are known worldwide, but perhaps the inn is most famous for its soups. The Hinshaws began canning their own soups in 1956. In 1973 NASA sent cans of Chalet Suzanne's Romaine soup to the moon on *Apollo 15* as part of the astronauts' food supply. The so-called Moon Soup has been on several missions since.

A key attraction of Chalet Suzanne is its proximity to what is perhaps Florida's most idyllic spot, Bok Tower Gardens. The 205-foot-tall, marble-and-coquina Bok Tower sits atop one of the highest ridges in Florida and is easily visible for miles around. Bok Tower Gardens is a 157-acre sanctuary with a Technicolor assortment of flowers, trees, plants, and more than 120 wild bird species. Built between 1922 and 1928, the gardens and the tower were the creation of magazine editor, author, and philanthropist Edward Bok.

CENTRAL EAST

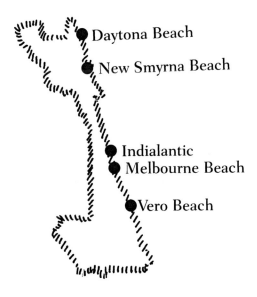

Daytona Beach

New Smyrna Beach

Indialantic
Melbourne Beach

Vero Beach

DAYTONA BEACH

Coquina Inn Bed & Breakfast
544 South Palmetto Avenue
Daytona Beach 32114
(386) 254-4969
(800) 805-7533
www.coquinainn.com

The four-room Coquina Inn is a 1912 coquina stone masonry, two-story house in Daytona's South Beach Street Historic District. Innkeepers Steve and Rhonda Hunt are dog people and have even referred to their inn as a "bed-and-biscuit." Two of their rooms are pet friendly (up to forty-five pounds).

Villa Bed & Breakfast
801 North Peninsula Drive
Daytona Beach 32118
(386) 248-2020
www.thevillabb.com

Boston marble quarry owner Bartholomew Donnelley built this Spanish Colonial hacienda on one and a half acres in north Daytona Beach in 1929. He would winter there in January and February only and then close it up the rest of the year. The house has arched entryways and windows, a red barrel-tile roof, and overhanging balconies. A black wrought iron fence surrounds lush grounds that would make any groundskeeper proud.

South Carolina bed-and-breakfast owner Jim Camp bought the compound in 1992 and had it listed on the National Register of Historic

COQUINA INN BED & BREAKFAST

Places. Both the house and grounds have been fastidiously restored. The Villa sits four blocks inland from the beach–close enough to walk but just far enough away to be away from the traffic–and is well suited to special occasions. (They were preparing for a wedding when I visited. Jim keeps a Rolls Royce available for just such an event.) The inn's interior is decorated with artwork, antiques, and Oriental rugs. The Villa has four regally appointed rooms, plus a separate Chauffer's Quarters suite. The upstairs King Juan Carlos Room opens onto a private rooftop terrace with its own hot tub.

VILLA BED & BREAKFAST

NEW SMYRNA BEACH

Night Swan Intracoastal Bed & Breakfast
512 South Riverside Drive
New Smyrna Beach 32168
(386) 423-4940
(800) 465-4261
www.nightswan.com

Chuck and Martha Nighswonger honeymooned at bed-and-breakfasts in Pennsylvania and New York, and that may have planted the seed for their purchase in 1989 of this stately, three-story 1906 Colonial Revival on the Halifax River. An architect from Philadelphia had built the house as his family's winter home. The Nighswongers spent two years renovating and converting it into a bed-and-breakfast. Then they purchased a second house (built in 1910) plus a carriage house next door, which they converted to a cottage. There are seven rooms in the Main House, seven more in the second house, the Cygnet House, and two suites in the Guest Cottage. Chuck and Martha have done an outstanding job of turning all three into a bed-and-breakfast destination while maintaining the integrity of the homes' era.

Riverview Hotel
103 Flagler Avenue
New Smyrna Beach 32169
(386) 428-5858
(800) 945-7416
www.riverviewhotel.com

A distinctive pink paint scheme, along with white trim and burgundy canvas awnings, makes the Riverview Hotel a standout, even on New Smyrna Beach's colorful Flagler Avenue. The three-story inn overlooks the Intracoastal Waterway and the Musson Memorial Bridge, which leads to the mainland. Captain S.H. Barber tended the Coronado Bridge (now the Musson Memorial Bridge) and in 1885 built what was then a two-story hunting and fishing lodge as well as his residence. In 1910 the building was jacked up into the air while a new lobby and dining room were constructed beneath it. He originally called it the Barber Hotel but later changed it to the Riverview.

During World War II, the hotel was a Coast Guard barracks, and it served as a youth hostel for a while in the 1970s, but like so many historic hotels in those decades, it fell into such disrepair that it had to be closed in 1980 because it had become a fire hazard.

In 1984 John Spang, owner of the Park Plaza Hotel in Winter Park, bought the boarded-up hotel. Spang renovated, added a pool

RIVERVIEW HOTEL

and dockside restaurant, and reopened the following year. In 1990 Jim and Christa Kelsey, who had owned the Faro Blanco Resort in Marathon, bought the Riverview from Spang. Christa Kelsey further renovated it, painting it the now-famous bright pink. In 2003 Jim and Christa's daughter Katie opened the spa next door. Sadly, in 2010 Christa Kelsey died suddenly of a heart attack. The Kelsey family, and Christa in particular, had become much-loved and very active members of the New Smyrna community, and Christa's passing came as a shock to the town. In 2011 the Kelsey family sold the Riverview to friends Judy and Wayne Heller, who had met the Kelseys when they stayed at the hotel fifteen years earlier. The Hellers have done a fine job continuing to run the Riverview as the Kelseys did for two decades.

The Riverview has eighteen rooms, four of which are suites. I stayed in the third-floor Coronado Suite. With horizontal board-and-batten wood paneling on the walls and ceiling and original heart-pine floors, it reminded me of a captain's quarters on an eighteenth-century sailing vessel.

INDIALANTIC

Windemere Inn by the Sea Bed & Breakfast
815 South Miramar Avenue
Indialantic 32903
(321) 728-9334
(800) 224-6853
www.windemereinn.com

Windemere Inn has three houses on serene Indialantic Beach. It's just a short walk across an access lane behind the houses to a gazebo and a boardwalk over the dunes to the beach. The three-story main house has five rooms, three with balconies that overlook the ocean. In addition, there is a spacious two-bedroom/two-bath carriage house, as well as a cottage with two more rooms and a two-room suite. Beth Fisher had worked as an innkeeper at the historic Greyfield Inn on Cumberland Island, Georgia, before purchasing the Windemere in

WINDEMERE INN BY THE SEA BED & BREAKFAST

1997. Beth's decorating has given the inn an atmosphere that is both elegant and inviting, striking a fine balance between luxurious and beach-comfortable.

In 2013 Jackie and Chuck Leopold purchased the Windemere from Beth Fisher.

MELBOURNE BEACH

Port D' Hiver Bed & Breakfast

201 Ocean Avenue

Melbourne Beach 32951

(321) 722-2727

(866) 621-7678

www.portdhiver.com

Walter Brown, a former instructor at the Kentucky Military Institute, and his wife, Elle Belle, had wintered in Melbourne Beach but moved to England for a while before returning with their new daughter, Diane, in 1925. The Browns bought a 1916 house just across the road from the beach that locals called the Pink House. Elle Belle changed that name to Port D' Hiver, or "Port of Winter" in French.

In 2003 Michael and Linda Rydson bought the house along with an adjacent carriage house and added two cabana houses behind it. They spent four years renovating the property, ultimately turning it into a boutique inn with an elegant Caribbean ambience.

In 2012 I met Michael, who took me on a tour of the tropically landscaped grounds and accommodations. The main house consists of the downstairs lobby and dining area, where breakfast and 5:00 P.M. wine and hors d'oeuvres are served, plus two rooms upstairs and one downstairs. All have French doors that open onto balconies or a porch. Then there are seven rooms (two are suites) in the Cabana houses, which wrap around a swimming pool and garden courtyard. The spacious, 525-square-foot Carriage House suite has its own Jacuzzi. All of the rooms are colorful and airy, and most have reclaimed hardwood floors, exposed-beam ceilings, private balconies, and whirlpool tubs. They remind me of luxury villas I have stayed at in St. Barts.

PORT D' HIVER BED & BREAKFAST

VERO BEACH

Caribbean Court
1601 South Ocean Drive
Vero Beach 32963
(772) 231-7211
www.thecaribbeancourt.com

Caribbean Court is a boutique hotel with eighteen rooms, a French-Caribbean restaurant, and a Havana-themed piano bar.

CARIBBEAN COURT

SOUTHWEST

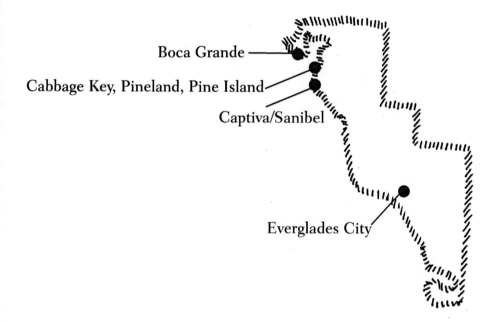

Boca Grande

Cabbage Key, Pineland, Pine Island

Captiva/Sanibel

Everglades City

BOCA GRANDE

Generations of Florida families have traveled to Boca Grande on Gasparilla Island for its relaxed island atmosphere and its world-famous tarpon fishing. Gasparilla Island is accessible only by a $6 toll bridge at its north end, by boat, or by seaplane. Its relative isolation has allowed it to maintain its tranquil, laid-back personality. There are no stoplights, and the only structure taller than three stories is a steel-girder 1927 lighthouse tower on the southern beach. The primary mode of transportation is electric golf cart. There's even a golf cart path that runs the length of the north end of the island into town.

For most of the 1800s, Gasparilla Island's few inhabitants were transient: mullet fishermen and a few rumrunners. But in 1885, phosphate was discovered in the middle of the state, and mining companies began transporting it by barge down the Peace River and out to Charlotte Harbor. As a result, Gasparilla Island, at the mouth of Charlotte Harbor, became a vital piece of property. The village of Boca Grande (Spanish for "big mouth," referring to Boca Grande Pass at the mouth of Charlotte Harbor) sprang up at the island's southern end to accommodate workers unloading phosphate from the river barges and reloading it onto ships sailing abroad. In 1907 the Charlotte Harbor and Northern Railroad replaced the river barges. Boca Grande became the railway's terminus and took on permanent status as a town.

Pirates such as Henri Caesar and Brewster "Bru" Baker frequented the southwestern coast of Florida and probably visited Gasparilla Island in the 1700s. However, this area's most famous pirate, José Gaspar, was a myth concocted out of tall tales told by an old Cuban fisherman, Juan "Panther Key John" Gomez, in the late 1800s. In 1918 the Charlotte Harbor and Northern Railroad released a publication entitled *The Gasparilla Story,* which pieced together some of Gomez's anecdotes. It also contained sales advertisements for railroad-owned residential property in Boca Grande. Those early property sales efforts turned out to be lackluster, but the romanticized fable of José Gaspar became accepted as genuine. The truth is that Gasparilla Island was likely named after a group of Spanish priests who ran a mission in Charlotte Harbor. Old charts that predate Gaspar's presumed lifetime by two hundred years show Gasparilla Pass as Friar Gaspar Pass.

ANCHOR INN

Anchor Inn
450 East Fourth Street
Boca Grande 33921
(941) 964-5600
www.anchorinnbocagrande.com

The Anchor Inn offers four accommodations—a one-bedroom suite, two two-bedroom suites, and a studio—all with full kitchens. The inn was built in 1925 and sits just a block from the center of town. I stayed in the one-bedroom suite and found it comfy and convenient. With large rooms, private entrances, a pool, and a perfect location, this a great place for families. "We're like a bed-and-breakfast without the breakfast," owner Sue Dutery told me. That's OK because there's lots of good food within easy walking distance, like Newlin's Mainely Gourmet next door (outstanding lobster roll sandwich) and Temptations, around the corner on Park Avenue.

Gasparilla Inn & Club
500 Palm Avenue
Boca Grande 33921
(941) 964-4500
(877) 403-0599
www.gasparillainn.com

Albert Gilchrist, who would become Florida's twentieth governor, was Boca Grande's first property owner to plat a neighborhood in Boca Grande. He also came up with the town's name. But it was Boston fertilizer magnate Peter Bradley who brought the town to life. While Gilchrist was planning Boca Grande, Bradley was buying up phosphate mining properties along the Peace River. In 1899 Bradley combined his assets to form the American Agricultural Chemical Company. In

GASPARILLA INN & CLUB

1907 he completed the Charlotte Harbor and Northern Railroad, with its terminus at Boca Grande, to replace the river barges that had been hauling his phosphate. Bradley then acquired Gilchrist's property in trade for company stock and began to develop the town. He built the railroad station, homes, and what would soon become Boca Grande's most regal edifice, the Gasparilla Inn. When it opened in 1913, it was a simple, twenty-room hotel, but within a year expansion was needed to accommodate its rapidly growing guest list.

Bradley hired father and son (and fellow Bostonians) Frank and Karl Abbott to run the hotel. For the dining room, the Abbotts shipped meat in from Boston and brought in fresh produce and tanks of drinking water from Arcadia on Bradley's railroad. They imported their seasonal staff from high-class hotels in the Northeast. The Gasparilla Inn quickly became an exclusive place for Boston socialites to vacation. It became so exclusive that the Abbotts began asking for social references before making a reservation. Names like DuPont, Drexel, and Eastman regularly filled the registry during its first two decades. But by 1930 the inn's luster had begun to fade. It had slipped into disrepair, and industrialist Barron G. Collier scooped up the bargain. Collier expanded the hotel once again, adding more rooms, a solarium, and the white-column front entrance that stands today.

Today the Gasparilla Inn is a classic resort in the tradition of the Barron Collier era, with a Pete Dye–designed golf course, tennis courts, swimming pools, and grand dining halls. The three-story hotel is painted bright yellow, with white trim and a burnt-orange shingled roof. Collier's two-story-tall white columns guard the front entrance. The main hotel has sixty-three rooms and suites. Seventeen additional quadruplex cottages, which can be opened up to accommodate families or groups, occupy several blocks in the surrounding neighborhood, adding seventy-four additional accommodations. Citrus trees, Australian pines, and towering palms grow throughout the grounds. The cottages are open year-round, but the main inn is open only from mid-October through Fourth of July weekend.

I stayed in one of the cottages. As soon as I opened the door to the sun porch, I recognized a wonderful aroma from my childhood: the smell of salt air–weathered wood. Like the rooms in the main hotel, the cottage was furnished and decorated in a charming and somewhat nostalgic 1950s' style.

Innlet
1251 12th Street
Boca Grande 33921
(941) 964-4600
www.theinnlet.com

At first glance, the Innlet, owned by the Gasparilla Inn, appears to be just a basic motel. But once you see inside the rooms, the first of two well-kept secrets is revealed. I stayed in one of the upstairs rooms that overlooks the inn's Intracoastal-side boat docks. It was bright and spacious—larger than the Gasparilla Inn's rooms—and it had a modern kitchenette. It was very comfortable for me, and it is ideal for visitors

INNLET

bringing their own boat. The other secret is the Outlet Restaurant at the Innlet, a locals' favorite for breakfast.

Palmetto Inn
381 Palm Avenue
Boca Grande 33921
(941) 964-0410
www.thepalmettoinn.com

Palmetto Inn was built as a home in 1900 and has been an inn since 1913. Owner Beverly Furtado welcomed me to wander through the inn, and it felt much like a visit to a friend's vacation home. It has just three suites—two one-bedrooms and one two-bedroom—that retain the inn's authentic century-old character.

PALMETTO INN

PINELAND, PINE ISLAND, CABBAGE KEY

Cabbage Key Inn
Intracoastal Waterway Channel Marker 60
Latitude 26 39 24.162 Longitude 82 13 20.635
Mailing address:
PO Box 200
Pineland 33945
(239) 283-2278
www.cabbagekey.com

First, rent a boat (unless you own one). That's the only way to get to Cabbage Key, a one-hundred-acre island in Pine Island Sound between Cayo Costa and Pine Island. I usually rent one from Jensen's Marina on Captiva Island, then motor north to Channel Marker 60 and turn left.

The first time I visited Cabbage Key, the dockmaster politely explained that only overnight guests or patrons of the restaurant are allowed to come ashore. "The island is self-sufficient, you know, and our septic tank can handle only so many visitors," he explained. I assured him that I was there for the famous Cabbage Key cheeseburgers, and he welcomed me ashore with a smile. It is widely rumored that this place was the inspiration for Jimmy Buffett's song "Cheeseburger in Paradise." I have heard the same rumor about the Le Select Bar and Grill in Gustavia on St. Barts in the Caribbean. Having sampled both, all I can say is that Cabbage Key has the tastier burger. Jimmy's not telling!

It's a short uphill walk from the dock to the "old house," now the inn and restaurant. The rustic, single-story pine home sits on top of a thirty-eight-foot-high Calusa shell mound. Inside, the walls, ceilings, and doorways are wallpapered with autographed and dated one-dollar bills hung by patrons. While you're there, it's worth another short

CABBAGE KEY INN

hike to the observation deck on the old wooden water tower, which offers a spectacular view of the island and surrounding Pine Island Sound.

In 1929 Alan and Grace Rinehart, son and daughter-in-law of famous detective/mystery novelist Mary Roberts Rinehart, purchased the then-uninhabited island for only $2,500. The retreat they built is now the Cabbage Key Inn and Restaurant. In addition to the restaurant and bar, the main inn has six rooms, plus there are seven rustic, 1930s' cottages tucked away around the island, ranging from one to three bedrooms. All have air-conditioning.

Cabbage Key Inn is now affiliated with the Tarpon Lodge on Pine Island (see next entry).

Tarpon Lodge
13771 Waterfront Drive
Pineland 33922
(239) 283-3999
www.tarponlodge.com

Pine Island, Florida's largest Gulf Coast barrier island, has seen some famous historical visitors. The most notable was Ponce de Leon, who careened his ship along the island's western shore to repair the ship's hull in 1513. He returned in 1521 and, during a skirmish with Calusa Indians, was shot with an arrow. His crew took him to Cuba to recuperate, but he ultimately died as a result of his wound. The Calusa had lived on Pine Island for a thousand years before Ponce de Leon arrived. They built huge shell mounds and dug elaborate canals across the island, but by the mid-1700s, they were all gone, wiped out by diseases brought by Spanish explorers, against which they had no immunity.

Thirty-foot-high hills, or shell middens, remain as evidence of the Calusa society. Some of the better preserved middens are near the community of Pineland on the northwest side of the island, where you'll also find, along the waterfront but well off the beaten path, the Tarpon Lodge.

The Tarpon Lodge's main lodge house and boathouse were built in 1926. An additional cottage and a stilt house came later. The lodge has nine rooms, and the stilt house twelve, while the boathouse has two bedrooms plus a kitchen. The cottage has one bedroom and a kitchen. It's not the easiest place to find, but those who do find it tend to come back year after year. This is the perfect launching point for some of Florida's finest coastal fishing. The waters of Pine Island Sound regularly yield snook, cobia, snapper, redfish, and the granddaddy of them all: tarpon.

SANIBEL, CAPTIVA

Remote Florida tropical islands, where you can truly "get away from it all" (but still arrive by car), are becoming a rare commodity. A couple of exceptions—Sanibel and Captiva Islands off the coast of Fort Myers—are hardy holdouts. To get any more remote, you will need a boat or a seaplane or be an exceptionally good swimmer.

Captiva's first permanent settlers arrived in the late nineteenth century. A hundred years before, the islands along Florida's southwest coast had been the hunting grounds and hideaways of pirates.

Do a little backroads exploring here and you'll eventually run across a quaint piece of Captiva history, the Chapel by the Sea. Captiva's earliest settler, William Binder, originally built the tiny white chapel on Chapin Road in 1901 as a schoolhouse. Binder was shipwrecked off Captiva in 1885 and was the first to file a homestead claim on the island. Next to the Chapel by the Sea is the Captiva Cemetery, shaded by gumbo-limbo trees. The high spot shared by the chapel and cemetery is an ancient Calusa shell midden.

Captiva Island Inn
11509 Andy Rosse Lane
Captiva Island 33924
(239) 395-0882
(800) 454-9898
www.captivaislandinn.com

Captiva Island Inn is a bed-and-breakfast made up of a collection of restored island cottages and duplexes on Andy Rosse Lane, Captiva's main street. The cottages are decorated in colorful Caribbean style and have Mexican tile floors and front porches with hammocks. There are twenty-one accommodations, from one-bedroom units to a five-bedroom house.

Captiva Island Inn

Castaways Beach & Bay Cottages
6460 Sanibel-Captiva Road
Sanibel Island 33957
(239) 472-1252
(800) 375-0152
www.castawayssanibel.com

Castaways consists of twenty-three assorted 1930s' clapboard cottages and duplexes containing forty accommodations that range from one-bedroom units up to three-bedroom cottages, all with kitchenettes or full kitchens. I've stayed here many times, and while these cottages are by no means luxurious, they are in a great location (just on the Sanibel side of the Blind Pass Bridge to Captiva) and include both beachfront and bayside units. The bayside units are a convenient place to dock and put in a boat (or, in my case, a kayak) to explore the island's wild mangrove coast. Again, don't expect luxury, but there's something rustically charming about the Castaways that keeps bringing me back.

'Tween Waters Inn
15951 Captiva Drive
Captiva Island 33924
(239) 472-5161
(800) 223-5865
www.tween-waters.com

The 'Tween Waters Inn sits roughly in the middle of four-mile-long Captiva Island, near its narrowest point between the Gulf of Mexico and Pine Island Sound. The inn has been a fixture here for three quarters of a century. Captiva's first homesteaders arrived in the late 1800s and early 1900s. One of them was Dr. J. Dickey from Bristol, Virginia. Dickey visited Captiva on a fishing trip in 1900 and returned

CASTAWAYS BEACH & BAY COTTAGES

'TWEEN WATERS INN

permanently with his family in 1905. Since there were no schools on Captiva, Dickey brought with him a tutor, Miss Reba Fitzpatrick. He built a schoolhouse with living quarters for Miss Reba upstairs. In 1925 Mr. and Mrs. Bowman Price, friends of the Dickeys from Bristol, purchased the schoolhouse and surrounding property. In 1931 they opened the 'Tween Waters Inn and shortly after began adding cottages to accommodate a growing list of visitors every winter. In the late 1940s, the Prices floated decommissioned Army barracks across the sound from Fort Myers, and they eventually expanded the schoolhouse, converting it into the Old Captiva House Restaurant.

The 'Tween Waters Inn remained in the Price family (daughter Dorothy took over in 1962) until 1969, when a Kentucky development group purchased the property with the intention of building condominiums. Thankfully, their project never came to fruition. It sold again in 1976 to Rochester Resorts out of Rochester, New York, which is still the current owner. Rochester Resorts restored the old cottages and the Old Captiva House Restaurant. The company also added five motel buildings, tennis courts, a marina, and a swimming pool. The 'Tween Waters has 102 hotel units and suites as well as 19 restored cottages and duplexes.

Some famous people made the 'Tween Waters their winter retreat. Anne Morrow Lindbergh, prolific author and wife of Charles Lindbergh, stayed there in the 1950s. She wrote one of her best known works, *Gift from the Sea*, while on Captiva. Jay Norwood "Ding" Darling, a 1930s' political cartoonist and later head of the U.S. Biological Survey and founder of the National Wildlife Foundation, also frequented the 'Tween Waters. He would rent two cottages, one to stay in, the other as his studio.

EVERGLADES CITY

Florida's Everglades is the largest subtropical wilderness in the United States, occupying much of the southern end of the peninsula. Technically, it is an immensely broad river. In some places, it's more than half the width of the state. This "river" trickles south, primarily out of Lake Okeechobee. With only a fifteen-foot drop in elevation from Okeechobee to Florida Bay, the flow is nearly imperceptible. Although most of the Everglades sits underwater, it is seldom more than a foot deep. Water evaporating from the Everglades supplies most of the rainfall in the southern portion of the state. Scientists call it the hydrologic cycle, a perpetual rain-generating machine. At one time, the Everglades system was considerably larger than it is now, but canals have drained and diverted much of the water from its northern and central sections to the state's heavily populated southeast coast.

Everglades National Park actually encompasses only the lower fifth—about 1.4 million acres—of the entire Everglades. The lower east-west stretch of U.S. Highway 41/Tamiami Trail marks the park's northern boundary. Another 720,000 acres on the north side of U.S. Highway 41/Tamiami Trail was designated the Big Cypress National Preserve in 1974.

Everglades City was industrialist Barron G. Collier's company town when he began construction on the Tamiami Trail. Later it would become the county seat. But after Hurricane Donna ravaged the area in 1960, Collier pulled his interests out. The county seat moved to Naples, and Everglades City settled into the sleepy fishing village that it still is today.

Everglades City gained some notoriety in the 1970s when it was an active airdrop point for South and Central American marijuana runners.

Everglades Historical Bed & Breakfast
201 West Broadway
Everglades City 38139
(239) 695-0013
www.evergladeshistoricalbedandbreakfast.com

Pat Bowen, owner of the Rod and Gun Club in Everglades City, purchased Barron Collier's old Bank of the Everglades, which ceased operations in 1962. Bob Flick and Patty Richards had operated On the Banks of the Everglades Bed & Breakfast there for a while, but it closed several years back. New owner Bowen has completely remodeled this Everglades City icon into a six-room bed-and-breakfast and spa.

Ivey House Bed & Breakfast
107 Camellia Street East
Everglades City 34139
(239) 695-3299
(877) 567-0679
www.iveyhouse.com

Ivey House Bed-and-Breakfast offers eighteen rooms in its inn, which was built in 2001, plus eleven more rooms and a restaurant in a restored, circa-1928 lodge that was once a boardinghouse for Barron Collier's Tamiami Trail construction crews. There's a two-bedroom 1920s'-era cottage as well.

EVERGLADES HISTORICAL BED & BREAKFAST

Rod and Gun Club
200 Riverside Drive
Everglades City 34139
(239) 695-2101
www.evergladesrodandgun.com

The original house that eventually would become the Rod and Gun Club was built by the city's founder, W.S. Allen, in 1850. Second owner George W. Storter enlarged it to accommodate hunters, sport fishermen, and yachting parties arriving in the Everglades in increasing numbers each winter season. In 1922 Barron Collier bought the lodge and operated it as a private club for his fellow industrial magnates and political dignitaries. Through the years, such luminaries as Herbert Hoover, Franklin D. Roosevelt, Dwight and Mamie Eisenhower, and Richard Nixon have been guests in the three-story, clapboard lodge on the banks of the Barron River.

The family of present owner Pat Bowen bought the historic

ROD AND GUN CLUB

structure in 1971 and has preserved the rustic atmosphere that was the Rod and Gun Club's hallmark in the 1930s, '40s, and '50s, but you don't have to be a president to stay there now.

Framed newspaper articles and photographs of famous visitors cover the walls in the lobby hallway. One photo shows a proud Robert Rand next to his trophy catch: a seven-and-a-half-foot, 187-pound tarpon caught in March 1939. Another is of Dwight and Mamie Eisenhower. Dwight is wearing shorts and a scruffy fishing hat. The grin on his face and the long rack of fish behind him indicate that he must have had a big day. The lobby itself is a trophy room. A five-foot-long sawfish bill, a gaping shark's jaw, a stretched alligator hide, deer and wild boar heads, and an assortment of game fish festoon the dark, wood-paneled walls. A stuffed raccoon keeps an eye on guests from its permanent perch behind the registration desk.

The rooms in the main lodge are no longer rented. Instead, there are seventeen accommodations in three cottage buildings on the north side of the property. The Rod and Gun Club restaurant in the main lodge serves seafood and steaks, as well as some Everglades specialties like gator tail and frog legs. The chefs will also gladly prepare your own fresh catch.

SOUTHEAST

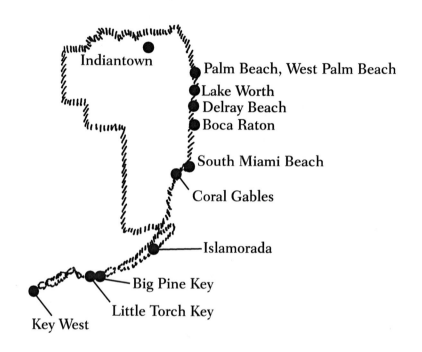

Indiantown

Palm Beach, West Palm Beach

Lake Worth

Delray Beach

Boca Raton

South Miami Beach

Coral Gables

Islamorada

Big Pine Key

Little Torch Key

Key West

INDIANTOWN

Seminole Inn
15885 Southwest Warfield Boulevard
Indiantown 34956
(772) 597-3777
www.seminoleinn.com

Seminole Indians settled here and operated a trading post in the early 1800s. Citrus growers and cattle ranchers moved into the area by the late 1890s. In 1913 the Army Corps of Engineers began building the St. Lucie Canal to connect the St. Lucie River (and its outlet to the Atlantic Ocean) to Lake Okeechobee. The canal passed just south of Indiantown, which made it an even more strategic trading location. Baltimore banker and president of what would later become the Seaboard Coastline Railroad, Solomon Davies Warfield, saw great potential in Indiantown as a major southern railway terminus. Around 1920 he bought several large tracts of land. He graded roads, built a train depot and a school, and had plans drawn up for a hotel. Construction on his Seminole Country Inn began in 1925, and it opened with considerable fanfare in 1926. Sadly, only seven months after the inn's opening, Solomon Warfield died, and so did his plans for converting Indiantown into a major rail hub.

An interesting piece of trivia: The hostess for the hotel's 1926 grand opening was Warfield's niece, Wallis Warfield Simpson. Ten years later, she would marry the Duke of Windsor, who passed up the opportunity to be king in order to marry her. The inn's two largest rooms are named for the duke and duchess.

Ownership of the Seminole Inn has bounced around over the decades. Homer Wall purchased it in 1974 and renovated it in 1975. He sold it and bought it back three times between then and 1993,

SEMINOLE INN

when his daughter and current owner, Jonnie Flewelling, bought it. Jonnie and husband Greg invested roughly $750,000 to restore the inn and upgrade the grounds—quite a leap from the $66,000 it cost to build the inn in 1926. The inn maintains its original character and Spanish Mission–style architecture, with parapet facades on the wings and barrel-tile roof over the central lobby. The dining room and lobby ceilings and walls, original to the structure, are made from pecky cypress harvested from the Allapattah Flats, a lowland bog that spreads out north of Indiantown. There is a large swimming pool, and the reception desk will arrange activities for guests, such as horseback trail riding, fishing on Lake Okeechobee, and touring the nearby Barley Barber Swamp. The Seminole Inn has twenty-two rooms, a swimming pool, and two restaurants: the casual Foxgrape Café and the Windsor Dining Room, popular for its Sunday brunch.

PALM BEACH

Florida's most expensive three blocks of shopping are on Worth Avenue in Palm Beach. For high fashion, fine art, and multi-carat diamonds, this is the place. Worth Avenue's first building, the Everglades Club, was built in 1918, and many buildings along the street were developed in the 1920s by renowned architect and developer Addison Mizner.

Mizner had his home apartment and offices in one of his buildings in the 300 block of Worth Avenue. Mizner, an eccentric by all accounts, had a pet spider monkey named Johnnie Brown, who rode on his shoulder almost everywhere he went. Follow the Via Mizner walkway (on the north side of the 300 block) to the first courtyard on the left and you will find Johnnie Brown's gravestone beneath a banana tree.

Brazilian Court Hotel
301 Australian Avenue
Palm Beach 33480
(561) 655-7740
www.thebraziliancourt.com

The Brazilian Court unobtrusively occupies an entire block between Australian and Brazilian Avenues in a quiet neighborhood three blocks west of the Atlantic Ocean and three blocks north of ritzy Worth Avenue. Looking very much like a Spanish hacienda, with its red barrel-tile roof, yellow stucco walls, and two open-air courtyards, this quietly elegant two-story (three-story with the penthouse suites) hotel has catered to Palm Beach regulars since it opened in 1926. That was what New York architect Rosario Candela had in mind when he originally designed it, and today's iteration holds true to his concept.

The "B.C." has had a variety of owners throughout its life. In the early 1930s, following Florida's real estate bust, it was sold at auction for a paltry $125,000 to the Mulford Realty Company, which made

BRAZILIAN COURT HOTEL

some additions, including the third-floor penthouse suites. It was sold again in 1963, 1978, and 1984, when it underwent an $8-million restoration.

Abraham Gosman purchased it in 1995 and remodeled extensively again, adding kitchenettes in each of its eighty studio and one- and two-bedroom suite rooms while maintaining the original cultured but comfortable ambience of the 1920s' Brazilian Court. Current owners Richard and Adam Schlesinger have added the option of condominium ownership with all of the same amenities offered by the hotel.

The Brazilian Court also has a fitness center, a full-service salon and spa, and the superb Café Boulud Restaurant, serving breakfast, lunch, and dinner. Impressive original artwork hangs in every hallway. One upper-floor wing features all Cubist art. Picasso would feel right at home.

I stayed in the second-floor west wing. My room, which overlooked the pool through a panoramic window, was quite plush without being ostentatious. Brazilian Court has some regular clientele who stay for a month—or two or three—and I can see that this is not only a wonderful place to stay, but it might also be a wonderful place to live.

Whereas the Breakers is grand and luxurious (see next entry), the Brazilian Court may best be characterized as intimate and luxurious.

Breakers Hotel
One South County Road
Palm Beach 33480
(888) 273-2537
www.thebreakers.com

In 1893 Henry Flagler bought property on the eastern shore of Lake Worth from Robert McCormick, one of the area's first settlers. Within weeks, crews began construction on the Royal Poinciana Hotel. Amazingly, they finished the colossal 540-room hotel in only ten months. Subsequent additions would bring the total rooms up to eleven hundred. At its completion, it was the largest wooden hotel in the world.

Palm Beach quickly turned into a popular resort for the affluent. The Royal Poinciana had tennis courts, croquet lawns, a golf course, and a mule-drawn trolley that shuttled guests to the Atlantic Ocean beach, less than half a mile away.

The beach turned out to be one of the biggest attractions, and that prompted Flagler to build a smaller, simpler hotel around an existing house right on the beach. It opened in 1896, and he named it the Palm Beach Inn. It was so popular that, within two years, it had to be enlarged. Everyone wanted to stay "down by the breakers." When he remodeled and added on again in 1901, Flagler decided to make the colloquialism official and changed the hotel's name to the Breakers.

Twice in its early history, the Breakers burned to the ground: first in 1903, during construction of yet another new wing, and then again

BREAKERS HOTEL

in 1925. A hair-curling iron, a recent invention, was blamed for that one.

The third and current Breakers (built from concrete this time, not wood) opened in 1926. The magnificent Royal Poinciana Hotel was dismantled in 1935, leaving the Breakers the sole Flagler-empire hotel in Palm Beach.

The Breakers Hotel is today, as it was then, the most opulent hotel in Florida's most opulent town. A long brick drive leads to its front, where architect Leonard Schultze chose to pattern the hotel's entryway after Rome's twin-towered Villa Medici. He also modeled the fountain in the center of the circular turnaround after one of the fountains in Boboli Gardens in Florence. Inside, the Breakers' cathedral-like lobby was inspired by another historic Italian structure, the sixteenth-century Great Hall of the Palazzo Carega in Genoa. Seventy-two artists were brought to the hotel from Italy to paint murals on the two-story-high, barrel-vaulted ceiling, lighted by eight crystal chandeliers hanging along its length.

The Breakers underwent a comprehensive $75-million renovation in the early 1990s. Then in 2006 a completely renovated pool and beachside area, which stretches across five finely landscaped acres on the south side of the hotel, was opened. This $15-million redesign took two years to complete and includes two new pools, a "relaxation" (adult) pool and an "active" (family) pool, bringing the total number of pools to five. At the far south end, twenty private, three-hundred-square-foot day bungalows are available for rent. They contain bathrooms, showers, refrigerators, and changing rooms. Two casual eateries are here as well: the Beach Club Restaurant and Bar and the Ocean Grill. In typical Breakers fashion, the pool and beachside areas are generously staffed and stocked with towels, robes, sunscreen, rafts—everything a beachgoer might need. Renovations are constantly ongoing, and in 2011 a five-year redesign of all of the guest rooms was completed. I stayed at the Breakers prior to the 2011 room upgrades, and they were plush then. I assume they are even more so now.

Today the Breakers sits on 140 acres of lush, manicured grounds and has 540 rooms, 68 of them suites, some as large as 1,700 square feet. Recreational offerings and amenities include two golf courses—the original Ocean Course (Florida's first eighteen-hole course) and a new Rees Jones course—ten tennis courts, a 20,000-square-foot spa and fitness center, a children's entertainment center, a croquet lawn, five swimming pools, and a half-mile-long private beach.

With nine restaurants, choices range from casual—burgers and salads at the poolside Ocean Grill—to exceptional fine dining at the Flagler Steakhouse or at the elegant HMF (for Henry Morrison Flagler) Lounge opened in 2012.

Palm Beach must have been Henry Flagler's favorite place, because he chose to make it his home from 1899 until his death in 1913. Flagler passed away at his cottage, which he had named the Nautilus, just up the beach from the Breakers. Mary Lily (Kenan) Flagler, his third wife, inherited most of his estate, including the Breakers. When Mary died in 1917, her family, the Kenans of Wilmington, North Carolina, took over operation of the hotel and continue to run it today.

Chesterfield Hotel
363 Cocoanut Row
Palm Beach 33480
(561) 659-5800
(800) 243-7871
www.chesterfieldpb.com

The Spanish-Mediterranean Revival–style Chesterfield Hotel blends discreetly into a residential neighborhood that borders tony Worth Avenue. There is no grand circular drive entrance with fountains, just a simple canopied doorway. The understated exterior hides an intimate and luxurious boutique hotel. The hotel staff is pleased to point out that, with only fifty-three rooms, the Chesterfield is the "smallest hotel in Palm Beach."

CHESTERFIELD HOTEL

When it opened in 1926 as the Lido-Venice Hotel, the hotel was touted as much for its fine restaurant as for its accommodations. Two years later, the name changed to the Vineta Hotel, which it remained for fifty years. Additions were made concurrent with changes in ownership in the 1930s, 1940s, and 1960s.

In 1977 new owners Leslie Raul and Fransesca Eszterhazy renamed the venue the Royal Park, and for a while the hotel and restaurant reflected their Hungarian heritage, but a couple of years later the hotel was converted into condominiums. In 1985 Lanny Horowitz and Carl Sax bought it, performed a $5-million restoration, and renamed it yet again to the Palm Court. Now it was a combination of condominiums, a hotel, and a restaurant.

In 1989 the Tollman-Hundley Hotel Group of Great Britain bought the hotel and, one more time, changed the name to the Chesterfield after another of the group's properties in London (which is named for sixteenth-century English statesman, author, and fourth Earl of Chesterfield, Philip Dormer Stanhope). Today the Chesterfield is part of the Red Carnation Hotel Collection, founded by Bea Tollman, which owns fifteen boutique hotels in Great Britain, South Africa, and Switzerland. The Chesterfield is its sole U.S. property.

The Chesterfield stakes its reputation on attention to detail in its amenities. It's a respite from the outside world for those of its guests who require it. It has been a private enclave for famous people such as Oscar de la Renta, Catherine Deneuve, Margaret Thatcher, Tony Bennett, Eartha Kitt, and Andy Rooney.

Throughout its history of multiple owners, this hotel has consistently maintained a fine gourmet restaurant. That tradition is carried on today in the Chesterfield's Leopard Lounge and Supper Club, a lavish dining room with hand-painted Lino Mario ceilings. It has also become one of Palm Beach's favorite nightspots.

WEST PALM BEACH

Casa Grandview Bed & Breakfast
1410 Georgia Avenue
West Palm Beach 33401
(877) 435-2786
www.casagrandview.com

The Casa Grandview was recommended to me by good friends who honeymooned there in 2012. Had they not told me about it, I likely wouldn't have found it—and it is an exquisite find. Although the grounds occupy about half a city block, it is well hidden behind palm trees and stands of bamboo in historic Grandview Heights, a 1920s' neighborhood of Craftsman and Art Deco bungalows and tree-lined

CASA GRANDVIEW BED & BREAKFAST

streets. Once you find its discreet brick entryway, Casa Grandview reveals itself as a micro-village, with brick pathways leading through a garden courtyard, a Spanish hacienda main house (it's actually two houses combined, one built in 1919, the other in 1925), eight cottages, a quadruplex cabana house, and two pools. With three suites in the main house, there are eighteen accommodations altogether. I stayed in the Sundance North Suite, which had a separate sitting room with a comfy, oversized leather couch and a credenza filled with books. Gracious hosts Cheryl and Kirk Grantham made me feel as if I were an old friend in their home. Breakfast was not a fixed menu. Kirk told me, "The kitchen's well stocked. We'll fix whatever you like." I enjoyed my guava pastry drizzled with chocolate sauce, then scrambled eggs, bacon, English muffins, and fresh-squeezed orange juice while the Granthams' sweetheart golden retriever, Rollie, rested at my feet.

Grandview Gardens Bed & Breakfast
1608 Lake Avenue
West Palm Beach 33401
(561) 833-9023
www.grandview-gardens.com

Grandview Gardens is another historic Grandview Heights neighborhood bed-and-breakfast. It includes four rooms in a 1925 Spanish-Mediterranean house, all with private entrances and all overlooking a garden courtyard and swimming pool. Two nearby vacation cottages are also available.

GRANDVIEW GARDENS BED & BREAKFAST

Palm Beach Hibiscus Bed & Breakfast
213 South Rosemary Avenue
West Palm Beach 33401
(866) 833-8171
(561) 833-8171
www.palmbeachhibiscus.com

Palm Beach Hibiscus comprises two 1917 houses relocated to West Palm Beach's hip City Place District in 1996. There are eight rooms, three of which are suites. The roomy Hibiscus Suite takes up the entire second floor.

PALM BEACH HIBISCUS BED & BREAKFAST

LAKE WORTH

Sabal Palm House Bed & Breakfast
109 North Golfview Road
Lake Worth 33460
(561) 582-1090
(888) 722-2572
www.sabalpalmhouse.com

The 1936 Sabal Palm House, across from Lake Worth Golf Course and adjacent to Bryant Park on the Intracoastal Waterway, was renovated and turned into a bed-and-breakfast in 1997. Current owners Colleen and John Rinaldi purchased it in 2002. There are four rooms in the main house, plus three rooms in the carriage house. Two of the rooms are suites.

SABAL PALM HOUSE BED & BREAKFAST

DELRAY BEACH

In the late 1980s, the citizens of Delray Beach decided that their downtown needed some help. The first step was to restore three historic buildings just off East Atlantic Avenue: the old Delray Beach High School, the 1926 Crest Theatre, and the 1913 Cornell Museum. They accomplished these three restorations in 1991, and this started the momentum to restore the surrounding area. Throughout the 1990s, East Atlantic Avenue, Delray's main street, and the Pineapple Grove Historic and Arts District, just north of the old schoolhouse, were completely revitalized. East Atlantic's new sidewalks, benches, and streetlights made it pedestrian friendly. Now East Atlantic is Delray's daytime and nighttime hot spot, with its concentration of boutiques, sidewalk cafés, coffee shops, and galleries.

Colony Hotel
525 East Atlantic Avenue
Delray Beach 33483
(561) 276-4123
(800) 552-2363
www.colonyflorida.com

The Colony is Delray Beach's oldest hotel, built in 1926 by Glassboro, New Jersey, hotelier Albert Repp. Its stucco exterior, arched entryways, and red barrel-tile, low-hipped roof are typical of the Spanish-Mediterranean Revival style that Addison Mizner made so popular in this region during Florida's 1920s' land boom. Martin Luther Hampton, an associate of Mizner's, designed it. Not so typical are the red domes that cap the Colony's twin cupola towers, which rise behind the lobby, and the second-floor aerial crosswalk that leads to the staff quarters behind the hotel. There is another interesting feature inside too. In a dining hall off the east end of the lobby, a latch in the room's

COLONY HOTEL

floor opens a hatch to reveal a staircase leading down to a cellar that was once the hotel's hiding place for liquor during Prohibition. It was being used as a wine cellar when I stayed there in 2000, and it's used for just storage now. Other pieces of nostalgia that have been retained include the original Otis manually operated elevator–the kind with a hand-closed metal gate and a mesh-reinforced glass door–and the hotel's original telephone switchboard.

The lobby has a tropical, Casablanca ambience to it: carpet runners over terrazzo floors, large potted palms and ferns, antique wicker furniture, and iron chandeliers from the 1920s. Two huge, semi-opaque skylights bathe the area in diffused light. Benny Goodman and Duke Ellington tunes float through the lobby and out the front door.

Charlie Boughton and his son George bought what was then the Alterap Hotel in 1935. They renamed it the Colony, and the family has owned and operated it since. Jestena Boughton is in charge these days. In 1988 she oversaw its refurbishing. She also owns another Colony Hotel in Kennebunkport, Maine. That one was built in 1914, and the Boughtons bought it in 1948. The Delray Beach Colony used to be open only during the winter and much of the staff worked for both hotels, traveling back and forth during the season change. Now it is open year-round.

The Colony has seventy rooms, including twenty-two two-bedroom suites. I stayed in the Seagrape Room, a two-bedroom suite on the third floor. It is cheerfully decorated in peach with white trim, and bright Florida-scene watercolors adorn the walls. Colony guests have access to the hotel's own private beachfront Cabana Club, complete with saltwater pool, lunch grille, and sunning deck.

HISTORIC HARTMAN HOUSE BED & BREAKFAST

Historic Hartman House Bed & Breakfast
203 Northeast 7th Avenue
Delray Beach 33483
www.twitter.com/HistoricHartman
(866) 787-2302
(561) 278-2302

In 2010 Jordan and Benita Goldstein purchased this 1923 two-story home in Delray Beach's Palm Trail neighborhood. They spent the next year completing a renovation started by the previous owner and adding an Olympic-size pool. Once the home of Delray Beach Assistant Postmaster Gustav Hartman, Historic Hartman House has four rooms.

OCEAN LODGE SUITES

BOCA RATON

Ocean Lodge Suites
531 North Ocean Boulevard
Boca Raton 33482
(561) 395-7772
www.oceanlodgeflorida.com

This 1950s-era motel, across from Boca Raton's South Beach, has been completely renovated and turned into the town's only bed-and-breakfast. All of the rooms have been converted into suites.

MIAMI BEACH: THE EARLY DAYS

One hundred years ago, the mosquito-infested mangrove key that would later become Miami Beach had virtually no beach at all. Locals referred to it simply as the Peninsula. It did have a thin sandbar connection to the mainland until 1924, when a storm washed it away. Two New Jersey farmers were the first to attempt to put down roots here. John Lum tried to grow a coconut palm grove in the 1880s, but he eventually gave up. John Collins, who had originally loaned Lum money for his coconut palm grove, arrived in 1909 and managed to successfully plant bananas, avocados, and mangos.

In 1910 flamboyant promoter, inventor, and auto industry tycoon Carl Fisher bought a vacation house across the bay from the Peninsula. Two years later, Fisher happened upon John Collins, who by then had begun construction of a bridge connecting the Peninsula to the mainland. Fisher negotiated a deal to finance the completion of the bridge in exchange for some of Collins' property. Fisher had the grand idea to cut down the mangroves and dredge sand from the bottom of the bay to build a resort city. But he drastically underestimated the cost of dredging. To the bewilderment of friends and business associates, Fisher plowed forward nonetheless, clearing the land and laying out the city. He poured millions of dollars into the project, which was incorporated as Miami Beach in 1915. Fisher had built a golf course, a yacht basin, and the Lincoln Hotel, but it wasn't catching on. He even tried offering free lots to those who would build on them. World War I further stalled the town's development, but in 1919, following the war's end, Fisher decided to add horse stables and a polo field to try to attract the wealthy. This would mark the turning point in what everyone until then had considered Fisher's colossal failure.

MIAMI BEACH REBORN

At times Ocean Drive on South Miami Beach looks like a giant outdoor fashion runway. It is flashy, loud, crowded, and sometimes just bizarre. But it beats the heck out of what it was in the early 1980s. What had decayed into a poor retirees' neighborhood in the 1970s had further deteriorated into a drug dealers' war zone by the early 1980s. Who could ever imagine that this place would be a vibrant community and a cultural and artistic crossroads? Well, Barbara Capitman did.

In 1976 the ever-myopic City of Miami passed a redevelopment plan to flatten everything south of 6th Street, the very southern tip of south Miami Beach. The rest would not be far behind. Towering high-rises separated by canals was the new concept—city officials' idea of a modern version of Venice perhaps? Thousands of low-income retirees would have been displaced. They may not have been young, but they still knew how to protest. The retirees managed to stave off the bulldozers long enough for Barbara Capitman to come along.

Capitman, a New York interior design journalist and magazine editor, immersed herself in the cause of saving south Miami Beach, some say to fill a void following her husband's recent death. At a cocktail party following an American Society of Interior Designers meeting in 1976, she and designer Leonard Horowitz concocted the idea of the Miami Design Preservation League. They shared a disdain for the latest direction of some of Miami's development—monstrosities like the Omni, for instance. They wanted to identify and preserve, from a design standpoint, what was unique and valuable to Miami. Right away they latched on to south Miami Beach's 1930s' Art Deco hotels, apartment houses, and storefronts.

The Miami Design Preservation League grew rapidly. Its first goal was to gain National Register of Historic Places status for the south Miami Beach Art Deco district. In 1978 Andrew Capitman, Barbara's older son, bought the aging Cardozo Hotel at 1300 Ocean Drive for $800,000, which he didn't have a penny of. To finance the venture, he structured and sold limited partnerships. It was a risky venture, but he pulled it off. At the time, no bank would touch property in south Miami Beach. Shortly after the Cardozo purchase, Andrew bought and renovated four more hotels. This broke the ice for the revitalization of the district.

In 1979 the Miami Design Preservation League won the designation of twenty blocks, approximately one square mile, of south Miami Beach to be listed on the National Register of Historic Places. The area is officially listed as the Miami Beach Architectural District. It was an unprecedented listing. This was the first designated historic district to be made up entirely of twentieth-century buildings. Most were Art Deco but some were Spanish-Mediterranean. No single building stood out from the others. Instead it was the sheer volume of buildings in one area—all built during a brief period and all reflecting one of two very distinct styles—that made this a unique place.

While the listing meant tax incentives for owners who renovated the buildings, it didn't guarantee that they couldn't be torn down. That would require a local historic preservation ordinance, and Capitman wasted no time getting to work on it. But it proved to be a much more daunting task than the national listing. Miami's city council, siding with condo developers, was adamantly opposed to it. A classic restoration-versus-new-development head-butting war took place, in the newspapers and in the courtroom, between Capitman and high-rise developers like Abe Resnick. Eventually some sections of the district were granted historic protection but not before several buildings were demolished, notably the 1940 New Yorker, the 1925 Boulevard, and the 1939 Senator.

By the mid-1980s, south Miami Beach was beginning to respond to resuscitation. Leonard Horowitz came up with an idea to breathe Technicolor life back into the buildings. He designed elaborate color schemes in bright pastels that emphasized the decorative features of their facades. This may not have been historically correct—in the 1930s they were mostly painted white with some green or beige trim—

but it was quite successful. Now these buildings, in all 33 Baskin-Robbins flavors, looked good enough to eat. It opened a lot of eyes and drew worldwide attention to the district. Suddenly south Miami Beach (or South Beach for short) was the place for outdoor fashion shoots. It was on the cover of every magazine in every grocery store. Oddly enough, it may have been the cheesy TV show *Miami Vice* that ultimately secured South Beach's popularity. The show began in 1984 and was shot regularly in Miami Beach. The bright Art Deco hotels on Ocean Drive were featured prominently in its opening credits.

Barbara Capitman's tireless efforts ultimately saved South Beach, but it didn't turn out exactly as she had planned. She and fellow Miami Design Preservation League members originally envisioned a district with distinct boundaries and buffer zones, with grand entrances and promenades. Still, no one can deny the extraordinary improvement to the district. The crusade consumed Barbara's life, drained her personal finances, and ultimately sapped her health, but she lived for it. One of her last great battles was to try to save the Senator Hotel at 12th Street and Collins Avenue. She succeeded in putting off its demolition for almost two years. Towards the end, she organized all-night candlelight vigils on the Senator's front porch. At one point she even chained herself to one of the columns. In late 1988 it was torn down and replaced with a parking garage. A year and a half later, one week before her seventieth birthday, Barbara Capitman passed away.

TROPICAL ART DECO IN MIAMI BEACH

Despite the Great Depression, south Miami Beach saw an explosion of development in the 1930s. During that decade, more than 2,000 homes, 480 apartment houses, and 160 hotels were built there. Most went up between 1934 and 1941. Among a handful of remarkably prolific architects and developers, three standouts—L. Murray Dixon,

Henry Hohauser, and Albert Anis—were responsible for the lion's share of these buildings. Dixon arrived in Miami Beach in 1928 from New York, where he had worked at the firm of Schultze and Weaver, designers of the Waldorf-Astoria Hotel in New York and the just-completed Biltmore Hotel in Coral Gables (Miami). Hohauser, also from New York, had worked in a firm with his cousin William Hohauser. While he was second to Dixon in quantity, Hohauser's designs are considered to be the most stylistic and elegant. Anis came from Chicago. All three were strongly influenced by the modern skyscrapers that were going up in their respective hometowns.

Art Deco was born of turn-of-the-century Paris fashion styles with some Italian and German influence thrown in. A 1925 exhibit of design, architecture, and applied arts in Paris called the Exposition Internationale des Arts Decoratifs et Industriels Moderns (Art Deco for short, although that term was not coined until the 1960s) showed the Moderne style to the world. Its intention was to shift design influences away from the "old" classic/Victorian/Revival styles. Twenty countries exhibited their finest modern designs. Although invited, the United States didn't participate, but some Americans did attend. One was Cedric Gibbons, then MGM Studios' supervising art director. He returned to the States so impressed by what he saw that he copied the style for many of MGM's movie sets, which was one of the ways that Art Deco gained wide exposure in the United States. In 1928 Gibbons designed one of the most recognizable Art Deco figures: the Academy Awards statue, the Oscar.

The new style reflected peoples' desire to emerge from the Depression and to put it behind them. It looked to a future of technological advances. Its arrival coincided with the big band/swing era and with the birth of commercial aviation. It was considered futuristic, fanciful, and optimistic. Two famous examples are New York's 1930 Chrysler Building and 1931 Empire State Building. The style wasn't just for skyscrapers, though. Gas stations and movie houses were popular Moderne subjects.

Ultimately the Moderne design trend influenced not only architecture but also automobiles, trains, ships, furniture, and even toasters and salt-and-pepper shakers. The style can be divided into a variety of substyles, among them Zigzag Moderne, which tends to be more ornamented and decorative; Depression Moderne, a more stark and simplistic style used frequently in the late 1930s and early 1940s for government buildings; and Streamline Moderne, my favorite. Streamline borrowed heavily from aerodynamics, wind-sculpted with all sharp angles rounded off. These buildings looked like they were going ninety miles per hour! They mimicked the sleek new trains, ocean liners, and airplanes. This was the Flash Gordon style.

Miami Beach Art Deco, or Tropical Art Deco, mixed in its own tropical flavor. Bas-relief sculptures and scenics etched in glass depicted pelicans, herons, flamingos, flowers, and palm trees. Local coral block was used frequently for window framing and archways. Nautical influences were common: porthole windows; wraparound, protruding "eyebrow" shades; stainless steel trim; ship railings; and decorative friezes with dolphins or waves. Architects paid homage to their favorite skyscrapers with soaring pylons or needlelike finials above entryways and stepped-back, segmented facades that gave the buildings a multidimensional look. These guys were one-man shows, choosing and designing every detail themselves, right down to the light fixtures. The Tropical Art Deco style continued in the interiors. Terrazzo floors, often tinted in various colors and poured in geometric patterns to match the decor, were common. Glass block was used strategically to let light (but not heat) into lobbies. Recessed and indirect lighting was popular. Builders would often hire local artists to paint elaborate murals if the budget allowed.

Miami Beach's building boom may have taken place despite the Great Depression, but it was not unaffected by it. Beneath their stylized facades, these were simple buildings of two, three, and occasionally four stories. Their stucco-on-block design was inexpensive to build. Working within the constraints of Depression-era economics, their designers were nonetheless determined to put up buildings, especially hotels, that had pizzazz and that conveyed a sense of optimism about the future.

A Miami Beach city ordinance declared the official start of the tourist season as December 16. All construction work had to stop by midnight December 15 so tourists could enjoy their visits in tranquility. There was always a feverish rush to complete construction by the deadline.

Miami Beach's biggest year was 1941, during which 41 hotels and 160 apartment buildings went up. It was also the last year of the building boom. Pearl Harbor brought it to a grinding halt. Most of the hotels were hastily converted to barracks for troops who trained on the beach.

SOUTH MIAMI BEACH

I could have listed thirty hotels here, but I decided instead to handpick half a dozen that I thought were significant.

Avalon Hotel
700 Ocean Drive
Miami Beach 33139
(305) 538-0133
(800) 933-3306
www.avalonhotel.com

Look for one of the hotel's signature 1950s-vintage cars parked out front: a Chevy Bel Air or Ford Thunderbird. The Avalon, built in 1940, was designed by Albert Anis. Now a property of the Atlantic Stars hospitality company, the Avalon exemplifies Miami Beach's Art Deco past.

CARDOZO HOTEL

Cardozo Hotel
1300 Ocean Drive
Miami Beach 33139
(800) 782-6500
(305) 535-6500
www.cardozohotel.com

Built in 1939, designed by Henry Hohauser, and named after Supreme Court Justice Benjamin Cardozo, the Cardozo was Andrew Capitman's first project, bought in 1978 and restored in 1979. Gloria Estefan and husband Emilio bought it and refurbished it in 1992. Its rounded corners and prominent eyebrows are classic Streamline Moderne. The 1959 Frank Sinatra movie *A Hole in the Head* was filmed there.

The Cardozo has thirty-nine rooms and four suites, all decorated in a modern style consistent with the Art Deco era but with the addition of horizontal teak paneling that adds considerable warmth. This was the first South Beach revival hotel and, I think, still one of the best.

CAVALIER HOTEL

Cavalier Hotel
1320 Ocean Drive
Miami Beach 33139
(305) 531-3555
www.cavaliermiami.com

A Roy F. France design, the Cavalier was built in 1936. Chris Blackwell, founder of Island Records (the late Bob Marley's label), bought and restored six hotels, including the Cavalier, on south Miami Beach in the mid-1990s.

Marlin Hotel
1200 Collins Avenue
Miami Beach 33139
(305) 695-3000
www.themarlinhotel.com

Chris Blackwell did a wild renovation in 1994 on this 1939 L. Murray Dixon Hotel. Its fifteen rooms are all designed around state-of-the-art audio-visual technology. The Marlin is also home to music recording studio South Beach Studios and is now part of the eclectic Mantis Collection of luxury boutique hotels.

MARLIN HOTEL

Tides Hotel
1220 Ocean Drive
Miami Beach 33139
(305) 604-5070
www.tidessouthbeach.com

The Tides is a nine-story-tall, L. Murray Dixon hotel. Built in 1936, it's very upscale, with forty-five expansive rooms and suites. The Tides became part of the New York–based King & Grove boutique hotel chain in 2012.

Victor Hotel
1144 Ocean Drive
Miami Beach 33139
(305) 779-8787
www.hotelvictorsouthbeach.com

The 1937 Hotel Victor is another L. Murray Dixon design. It reopened in 2003 with eighty-eight rooms, following a $48-million renovation overseen by architect Jacques Garcia. It is owned by San Francisco-headquartered Commune Hotels and Resorts, the result of a merger between Thompson Hotels and Joie de Vivre in 2011.

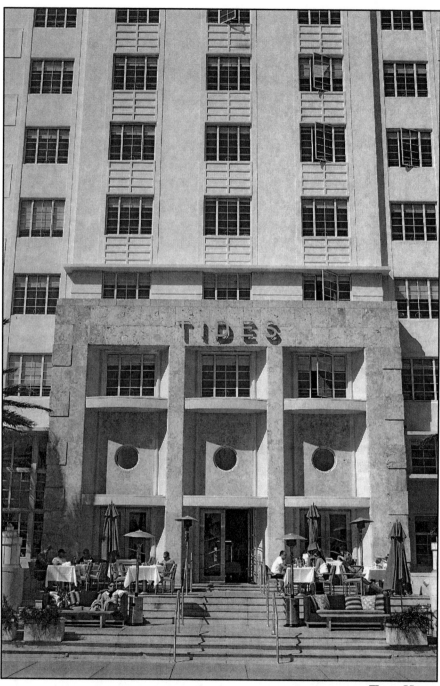

TIDES HOTEL

VICTOR HOTEL

CORAL GABLES

Historians describe George Edgar Merrick variously as a dreamer, a poet, a schemer, a philanthropist, a visionary, a darn good salesman, an extraordinary success, and a crushing failure. He was all of those things. George was twelve when his father, Reverend Solomon Merrick, moved the family from Massachusetts to Florida. It was 1898, and Reverend Merrick had chosen a farm a few miles south of the land that Julia Tuttle had split with Henry Flagler two years earlier. The Merricks did well in citrus farming. Solomon Merrick built the family a large house from locally mined oolitic limestone, which he mistakenly referred to as coral when he named their home Coral Gables. When his father died in 1911, George inherited the farm.

George Merrick wasn't all that excited about farming. His vision was to design and build the perfect planned city. He began acquiring land around the family homestead. With the help of his uncle Denman Fink, architect Phineas Paist, and landscape architect Frank Button, the grand community of Coral Gables came to life, at least on paper. While he had garnered some financial backing, Merrick needed to pre-sell many lots to finance the whole venture. Fortunately, Merrick knew how to promote. The lots sold almost as fast as they were put up for sale, many sight unseen. Through a combination of good timing and clever marketing, Merrick's plan was a success, and he built the city of his dreams. It had (and still has) beautiful parks, tree-lined boulevards, its own university (the University of Miami, which opened in 1926), and something quite novel for its time: very strict building codes and architectural restrictions.

Biltmore Hotel
1200 Anastasia Avenue
Coral Gables 33134
(855) 311-6903
www.biltmorehotel.com

The last great addition to Merrick's Coral Gables was the majestic Miami Biltmore Hotel. Begun in 1924 and completed in 1926, the fifteen-story (including its tower) hotel was the result of a partnership with Biltmore Hotels chain owner John McEntee Bowman. The grandeur was short lived, however. In September of 1926, a devastating hurricane struck Miami head-on. The new town was pummeled by 130-mile-per-hour winds. Three years later, the stock market crash finished the job the hurricane had started. Merrick was completely wiped out.

George Merrick left Coral Gables and drifted down to the Upper Keys, where he ran a fishing camp until it was demolished by the 1935 Labor Day hurricane, the most powerful ever to strike North America. Merrick returned to Miami and at first dabbled in real estate again. Then, from 1940 until his death in 1942 at age fifty-six, he was postmaster of Miami.

Sometimes a person's life must be viewed many years in retrospect to judge whether he was a success or a failure. George Merrick's dreams did come true, although some came to fruition years after he was gone. Coral Gables turned into the beautiful community he had envisioned. No doubt the University of Miami far exceeded his expectations. Perhaps some of the most important things he left behind were his city planning ideas and design philosophy, still considered the textbook model for developers today. Lastly, there's the Biltmore Hotel. Although it cycled through some rough times and was almost slated for demolition in the 1970s, today the Biltmore is everything Merrick wanted it to be and more.

BILTMORE HOTEL

The Miami Biltmore was a $10-million project when construction began. (Remember, that's in 1920s' dollars.) Trainloads of guests came from up and down the Eastern Seaboard to attend its 1926 grand opening. The Biltmore positioned itself as host to the elite—British royalty, Hollywood movie stars, politicians, and wealthy industrialists—but it was up against tough times. The 1926 hurricane and the stock market crash of '29 took their toll. Then in 1931, following John McEntee Bowman's death, the Biltmore Hotel chain filed for bankruptcy. Despite these circumstances, the Miami Biltmore managed to remain open throughout the 1930s. In an attempt to attract what clientele they could during the Depression, the hotel's owners hosted swimming exhibitions in their giant 21,000-square-foot swimming pool. A young Johnny Weissmuller was swimming coach there for a while and actually broke a world swimming record in the Biltmore pool.

During World War II, the hotel was converted into an Army Air Forces regional hospital. After that, it was a Veterans Administration hospital until 1968, when it closed its doors. The Biltmore remained boarded up throughout the 1970s. The City of Coral Gables had gained ownership through the Historic Monuments Act and Legacy of Parks Program, but nothing was done with it until 1983, when the city began to refurbish it. It took four years and more than $50 million to complete the major restoration. On New Year's Eve in 1987, the Biltmore reopened. Three years later, it closed again. In 1992 Seaway Hotels bought it and reopened it after completing yet another restoration costing $40 million. This time it seems to have worked.

Among other improvements, Seaway added a health club and spa. Today's Biltmore is just what George Merrick hoped it would be. It is a grand and luxurious Spanish-Mediterranean hotel, with a Spanish barrel-tile roof and a center tower that was patterned after the Giraldo Tower in Seville, Spain. It has a lush, gardenlike courtyard with a central fountain, all overlooking the Coral Gables Golf Course. The ornate main ballroom, with its towering stone columns, is suitable for entertaining royalty. In 1996 the National Register of Historic Places designated the Biltmore a national historic landmark.

The Biltmore has had its share of famous guests throughout its on-again, off-again lifetime, including the Duke and Duchess of Windsor, Bing Crosby, Judy Garland, Douglas Fairbanks, Lauren Bacall, Robert Redford, and Barbara Bush. The most infamous was Al Capone, who stayed in the tower suite (now called the Presidential, or Everglades, Suite but better known as the Capone Suite) while hiding out from law enforcement officials.

The Biltmore has 275 rooms, 130 of which are suites. The two-bedroom Everglades Suite is on the thirteenth and fourteenth floors. Everglades scenes are painted on its domed ceiling. It has its own kitchen, Jacuzzi, and stone fireplace. The Penthouse/Merrick Suite occupies the entire fifteenth floor. It has three bedrooms and baths, a fireplace, and two balconies to take in the best views at the hotel. The Biltmore has four restaurants: Palme D'or for elegant French dining; Fontana in the courtyard where they serve Sunday brunch; the casual, poolside Cascade; and the golf course's 19th Hole Grill.

Hotel St. Michel
162 Alcazar Avenue
Coral Gables 33134
(305) 444-1666
www.hotelstmichel.com

The three-story Hotel St. Michel was originally designed as an office building by architect Anthony Zink, who had come to Miami from New York in 1925. Shortly after it opened in 1926, the upper two floors were converted into hotel rooms while the first floor was retained as retail space. It was called the Hotel Sevilla until the 1960s, when the name changed to the King Richard Inn. In 1979 it changed again, this time to Hotel Place St. Michel.

Dark wood floors, hand-painted Spanish tile work, and the original brass, manually operated elevator give the twenty-eight-room Hotel St. Michel (they have dropped the Place) a bit of Old World charm.

THE KEYS: FLAGLER'S LAST FRONTIER

Former Standard Oil Company cofounder and railroad and hotel magnate Henry M. Flagler was already seventy-five years old in 1905 when he began construction to extend his Florida East Coast Railroad beyond the southern reaches of Florida's mainland. Most people considered the idea of building a 150-mile railroad that would skip across tiny coral islands and be elevated over water merely the preposterous dream of a crazy old man. But when word came that a shipping canal would be dug across Panama, Flagler decided that his railroad must go all the way down to Key West. It would be the nearest rail terminal to the canal by three hundred miles. It took seven years to build—four longer than first estimated—but on January 22, 1912, the first official train arrived in Key West with eighty-two-year-old Henry Flagler aboard. Fifteen months later, he died. Arguably, Flagler's Over the Sea Railway still stands today as Florida's most astounding engineering feat.

The Florida Keys are a one-hundred-mile-long string of islands that sit atop the only living coral reef in the continental United States. The Keys are connected by one road, U.S. 1, which ends at Key West. The ambience in the Keys is so foreign that they could be their own country. Key West attempted to be just that in 1982, when residents declared secession from the United States and adopted the name Conch Republic following a federal drug-search roadblock that stopped all traffic to and from the islands for a week.

Native-born Keys' residents call themselves Conchs. The term dates back to the arrival of the Upper Keys' early pioneers, who came from the Bahamas. In the 1780s, many British Loyalists who had fled the United States following the American Revolution settled in the Abacos, the northernmost of the Bahamian out-islands. In the mid-1800s, descendants of these Loyalists sailed from there to Upper Matecumbe (now known as Islamorada) in the Upper Keys and resettled. They were quiet and simple-living people who built their homes from driftwood, planted pineapple and Key lime groves, and fished. Conch, a large shellfish plentiful in these waters, was a staple in their diet, and the nickname stuck. Eventually the name evolved to include anyone born in the Florida Keys.

Devastation came to the descendants of those pioneers on Labor Day in 1935, when what experts consider the most powerful hurricane ever to strike the continental United States blasted across the islands. Although small in diameter, the storm was horrifically potent, cutting across Long Key and Upper and Lower Matecumbe Keys with gusts estimated near 250 miles per hour. A twenty-foot tidal wave swept over the islands and ripped whole buildings off their foundations. The residents had almost no warning. On Sunday, the day before it struck, forecasters had called it a mere tropical storm and predicted that it would likely pass south of Key West.

The Labor Day hurricane wiped out whole generations of pioneer families who had settled the Upper Keys, mostly Russels, Pinders, and Parkers. It also killed hundreds of road workers—all World War I veterans—camped on Upper and Lower Matecumbe. In the summer of 1935, the Veterans Administration had employed 680 World War I veterans to work on building the Overseas Highway (U.S. Highway 1) down to Key West. That weekend some workers had gone to Miami for the holiday, but many stayed behind in their temporary camps. The storm intensified dramatically overnight, and on Monday morning officials called for a train from Miami to evacuate the road workers and residents. The eleven-car passenger train reached Matecumbe right when the wall of water struck, blasting each of its one-hundred-ton cars right off the tracks. Only the locomotive remained upright.

It would be the last train to travel those tracks. The hurricane's death toll exceeded four hundred and included all of the road workers who had remained in the camps along with local residents. Months after the storm, remains of victims' bodies were still being recovered. Thirty years later, while dredging on an outlying key near Islamorada, a developer found an automobile with a 1935 license plate and five skeletons inside.

Key West is the westernmost (as well as the southernmost) of the Florida Keys, so the name seems geographically appropriate. However, it is likely that the name Key West is really a mispronunciation of Cayo Hueso, Spanish for "Island of Bones." Eighteenth-century Spanish fishermen reported finding piles of human bones on the island's shore. Most historians believe that these were the remains of a band of Calusa Indians who lost a terrible battle to either Tequesta or Carib Indians.

For reasons that have never been clearly explained, Spain deeded the island of Key West to a Spanish military officer named Juan Pablo Salas in 1815. In 1822, just after the United States had acquired Florida from Spain, Salas attempted to sell the island simultaneously to two different people. First he traded it to a ship captain named John Strong, purportedly in exchange for the captain's sloop. Second, in a bar in Havana, he sold it to a Mobile, Alabama, businessman named John Simonton for $2,000. Simonton won the ensuing dispute over ownership and immediately sold off three-quarters of the island: one quarter to John Fleming, his friend and business associate, and the other two quarters to John Whitehead and Pardon Greene. The four owners were Key West's first developers, opening a salt mine and importing cattle and hogs. They also recognized its importance as a port and a strategic military location. Simonton invited the United States Navy to consider building a base there but ended up with more than he bargained for. The Navy built the base and put it under the command of Commodore David Porter to counter pirates who frequented the surrounding waters. Porter promptly declared himself the virtual ruler of Key West, appropriating equipment and property without permission whenever he wished. He was considered a tyrant, but by 1826 he had indeed driven the pirates out of the surrounding seas.

By the early nineteenth century, the waters around Key West had a burgeoning industry: salvaging the cargoes of ships smashed on the outlying reefs. Most of the earliest so-called wreckers were transients from the Bahamas and Cuba, but following the War of 1812, some small groups of New Englanders from Connecticut and Rhode Island settled permanently in Key West. Wrecking was extremely dangerous work and the mortality rate was high, but brave Key Westers could make a healthy living at it, typically retaining at least half the value of the salvaged cargoes. In 1828 the United States courts stepped in to regulate it. Wreckers and their ships had to be licensed. A maritime court established in Key West decided how the proceeds of salvages were disbursed. This did not, however, stifle the wrecking industry. In fact, this was the beginning of Key West's golden era. From the 1830s through the 1840s, Key West may have been the richest city per capita in the United States. But it would not last forever. In the 1850s, the United States government began erecting lighthouses along the reefs in the Keys to prevent shipwrecks, and the industry faded. The Wrecking License Bureau finally closed in 1921.

For much of its history, Key West has attracted artists and writers, among them John Audubon, Robert Frost, Tennessee Williams, Thomas McGuane, Hunter S. Thompson, Jimmy Buffet, and Key West's most famous resident writer, Ernest Hemingway, who lived on the island from 1928 to 1940. Between afternoon fishing expeditions and all-night bar excursions, he produced some of his best-known work, including *A Farewell to Arms* and *To Have and Have Not*.

Key West manages to reinvent itself time and again. Sponging, cigar making, fishing, tourism, even treasure hunting have all been industries that have kept the island afloat. Today Key West is a mix of tacky tourism and well-preserved history. (The well-preserved part isn't easy when you're in the crosshairs of hurricane territory.) Old Town, the western end of the island, is colorful and eclectic. Side street neighborhoods are made up of hundred-year-old pastel Conch houses that owe much of their architectural style to the woodworking skills of turn-of-the-century boatbuilding craftsmen, who occasionally incorporated salvaged pieces from wrecked ships into homes. You may not need a passport to get there, but the whimsical Conch Republic is its own world, an outpost for individuals, and a monument to resilience.

ISLAMORADA

Cheeca Lodge & Spa
81801 Overseas Highway
Islamorada 33036
(305) 664-4651
(800) 327-2888
www.cheeca.com

In the northern Upper Keys, visitors find some of the best big-game fishing and scuba diving in the world. It's difficult to get off the beaten path down there since there is only one path from Key Largo south: U.S. Highway 1, also known as the Overseas Highway. However, this makes it easy to give directions using mile markers. Add two digits to the end of the mile marker number, and that's the street address.

At mile marker 81.8 stands the 1935 Hurricane Monument. It's also a tomb that contains the cremated remains of some of the storm's victims. A plaque at the base of the twelve-foot-tall, coral keystone monolith reads, "Dedicated to the memory of the civilians and war veterans whose lives were lost in the hurricane of September Second 1935."

Entrance to the historic Cheeca Lodge is right next door to the

CHEECA LODGE & SPA

monument. Its original owner, Clara Downey, called it the Olney Inn (after her hometown of Olney, Maryland) when she opened it in 1946. There were just twenty-two cottages then. One of the Olney Inn's earliest guests was President Harry Truman. This likely set the stage for the resort becoming a popular retreat for politicians, sports figures, and movie stars for decades to come. The name changed to Cheeca Lodge in the 1960s when Cynthia and Carl Twitchell purchased it, adding the lodge, ocean-front villas, and a golf course. "Chee" was Cynthia's nickname, and the "ca" came from Carl. In 2005 the entire complex underwent a $30-million renovation, and in 2009 the main lodge had to be rebuilt following a New Year's Eve fire.

Among the first buildings the original Conch settlers built on Islamorada were a church in 1890 and a schoolhouse in 1900 on property that is now part of the Cheeca Lodge compound. Next to the church, they established a small cemetery. The 1935 hurricane destroyed the schoolhouse and the church, but the Pioneer Cemetery remains. Looking out of place among the beach loungers and Hobie Cats, the tiny cemetery is surrounded by a low, white picket fence. Only eleven gravesites are marked, but there are more without names. In the center, a life-size statue of an angel marks the grave of Etta Dolores Pinder (1899–1914). Tossed a thousand feet in the mighty winds of the 1935 hurricane, the angel, with one wing broken and a hand missing, nevertheless stands tall. A historical marker in one corner of the cemetery reads: "This cemetery memorializes the determination and vision of over fifty pioneer Anglo-Bahamian Conchs who labored to settle and organize the first community on Matecumbe Key. Descendants of three pioneer families, the Russells who homesteaded in 1854, the Pinders in 1873, and the Parkers in 1898, are buried on this land."

The Cheeca Lodge fronts a quarter mile of beach and has 214 rooms, suites, and villas; three restaurants; and its own nine-hole golf course. In 2011 New York hotel and commercial property group Northwood Investments purchased the Cheeca Lodge for a reported $100 million.

Big Pine Key

Barnacle Bed & Breakfast
1557 Long Beach Drive
Big Pine Key 33043
(305) 872-3298
(800) 465-9100
www.bandbontheocean.com

Big Pine Key is decidedly quieter and more leisurely than its famous neighbor thirty-five miles to the south. That's what I was looking for back in 1999 when I found the Barnacle Bed & Breakfast, a place where leisure has been refined to an art form.

Long Beach Road looks a little like it's being reclaimed by the native flora. A simple limestone wall marks the Barnacle's entrance. Don't mistake this for a luxury resort. The Barnacle is not a spa. It's a respite. Think of it as visiting a very eccentric friend's house on a remote beach.

This place is an architectural enigma. Its style doesn't fall neatly into any conventional category. Modern? Eclectic? Nautical? Tropical? There are no right angles. Its pipe railings, archways, and open-air balcony space remind me of a beached ocean liner, albeit with an exterior painted in varying shades of earth tones reminiscent of the 1970s. From the top floor sunrise-watching deck (the ocean liner's bow), guests can scan the Atlantic's vivid turquoise water for rolling dolphins or maybe a jumping manta ray.

I have stayed in both upstairs and downstairs rooms. There is creative use of space for bathrooms and tiny kitchenettes, with the walls skewed at odd angles. Multicolored tile and stained glass add a wide spectrum of color.

Original owner Steven "Woody" Cornell designed and built the

Barnacle in 1976. Dive operators Tim and Jane Marquis bought it from Woody in 1994. "We didn't see any reason to change much of anything that Woody had built," Jane explained in her casual Louisiana accent. "I don't know how Woody came up with the design for this place, but it is definitely an original. Tim and I had been coming down here for years before we bought this place. We love it. It's quiet, laid back, not rush-rush. We had been in the scuba diving trip business for years, and buying the Barnacle turned out to be the perfect complement. We can combine a stay here with customized dive packages—out to Looe Key or wherever the customer wants to go—or with fishing trips. We also own five boats. Business is mostly through word of mouth and our website."

If Tim and Jane's house is an ocean liner, their beach is a tropical port of call. Five steps outside my room, coconut palms, with hammocks strung between them, line the shore. More hammocks swing in the breeze under a thatched-roof hut. Tim and Jane offer

BARNACLE BED & BREAKFAST

all kinds of exploration amenities for their guests—kayaks, canoes, sailboats, fishing trips, dive trips—but I chose an early afternoon nap in a hammock.

When I last visited in 2012, Tim and Jane's son Eric prepared a tasty breakfast of fresh orange juice and waffles with strawberries, blueberries, and raspberries, served alfresco on the Barnacle's second-floor deck. The Barnacle has three rooms, one upstairs and one downstairs in the main building, plus a cottage behind the main building.

LITTLE TORCH KEY

Little Palm Island Resort and Spa
28500 Overseas Highway
Little Torch Key 33042
(305) 872-2524
www.littlepalmisland.com

What if Gilligan's island had had air-conditioning, a gourmet restaurant, a health spa, and a scuba diving shop and boat, and you could share it all with a handful of friends? Little Palm Island Resort and Spa, three miles out in the Atlantic Ocean off Little Torch Key, is just such a place. It's what Thurston Howell III would really have preferred.

It used to be called Sheriff's Island when John Spottswood, sheriff of Monroe County and later a Florida senator, owned it. President and Mrs. Harry Truman were regular guests back then. It evolved into a private fishing camp for statesmen and other VIPs. In addition to the Trumans, the Roosevelts, Kennedys, and Nixons were all guests at one time or another.

Restaurateur Ben Woodson, along with a group of investors, purchased the island in 1986 and built the Little Palm Island Resort, which opened in 1988. It is now part of the Noble House Hotel and Resorts Group out of Kirkland, Washington.

This lima bean–shaped, 5-acre island has 30 suites—ranging in size from 550 to 1,000 square feet—in bungalows with genuine palm-thatched roofs, indoor/outdoor showers, and private decks. From the outside they appear island rustic, like huts on Fiji or Palau. Inside they are elegant and luxurious, if not Hemingway-like—king-size four-poster beds with mosquito-net canopies (for ambience only), British Colonial furniture, and, of course, air-conditioning. There are, however, no phones, televisions, or alarm clocks in the rooms. If you insist on checking in with your office, Harry Truman's old outhouse has been converted into a phone booth.

Little Palm Island is perhaps a bit more South Pacific than Florida-Caribbean in appearance. A natural white-sand beach—rare in the Keys and deposited by rapid currents in Newfound Harbor Channel—wraps around one end. Coconut palms lean out over the sand and the emerald waters. Hibiscus, oleander, and bougainvillea grow wild everywhere. Back in 1962, Warner Brothers filmed the movie *PT 109,* which was set in the South Pacific, on Little Palm Island.

Less than five miles away is Looe Key National Marine Sanctuary, one of the most beautiful underwater spots in the Keys. The Little Palm Island dive shop operates two thirty-foot boats for diving at Looe Key and on the *Adolphus Busch,* a sunken freighter. Other activities include day and moonlight sailing charters on a forty-two-foot yacht, deep-sea and flats fishing, and seaplane excursions. Or you can spend a few hours at Little Palm Island's full-service spa and fitness facility.

Little Palm Island Resort is not an inexpensive place, but it is considered by many travel experts to be Florida's ultimate getaway. Who knows? While you're there you might run into Ginger, Mary Ann, or the Professor.

KEY WEST

Artist House
534 Eaton Street
Key West 33040
(305) 296-3977
(800) 582-7882
www.artisthousekeywest.com

One of the most photographed houses in Key West is the charming Victorian Artist House, built in 1898 by pharmacist Thomas Otto and his wife, Minnie. Charming, yes, and creepy too. The gingerbread-laced wraparound porches and third-story turret give it the appearance of a life-size dollhouse—and apparently it was. The Otto's son, Robert Eugene (Gene for short), was born there in 1900. The quite wealthy Otto family employed servants, one of whom was a nanny who may have come from Jamaica or the Bahamas and may have practiced voodoo. Mrs. Otto became disgruntled with her and fired her. Upon her departure, the nanny gave four-year-old Gene a doll dressed like him named Robert. Young Gene became extremely attached to Robert. Reportedly he carried him everywhere and had long conversations with him. He also blamed Robert for all manner of mischievous occurrences in the house, including tearing up his other toys. Some reports claimed poltergeist activity in the house as well: furniture moving, doors opening and closing on their own, and the like.

Gene grew up to become an accomplished painter, studying in Chicago and living and working in Paris. After his parents died, Gene, along with his wife, Anne, whom he had met in Paris, returned to Key West. They moved back into the house, where he turned the seven-window turret room into his artist's studio. Gene still had Robert. He

ARTIST HOUSE

propped the doll up in one of the turret windows so he could look out over Eaton Street. Passersby said that sometimes Robert would turn his head and watch them walk by. They also said that it seemed his facial expressions would change. Gene Otto died in 1974, Anne in 1976. Robert now resides at Key West's Civil War Fort East Martello Museum, which hired Gene Otto to design its gallery space.

Today Artist House is a seven-room inn that showcases its classic Queen Anne Victorian style, with twelve-foot ceilings, artfully carved crown moldings, and etched glass transoms. The most fascinating room, of course, is the Turret Suite. Its second-floor bedroom has a sitting area, two baths, French doors that open onto a balcony, and a winding staircase leading to the third-floor tower, with its own bed surrounded by seven windows.

It seems that Robert's antics moved with him to the museum, but some believe the ghost of Anne Otto is still in the house.

Authors of Key West Guesthouse
725 White Street
Key West 33040
(305) 294-7381
(800) 898-6909
www.authorskeywest.com

Authors Guesthouse is three structures: a circa-1910 house with ten rooms, plus a pair of cottages. It has a private, tucked-away atmosphere. The rooms are named for famous writers and other notables who have visited or resided in Key West. Authors Guesthouse is owned by Diane Hadley and Landon Bradbury, who also own the Blue Parrot Inn.

Avalon Bed & Breakfast
1317 Duval Street
Key West 33040
(305) 294-8233
(800) 848-1317
www.avalonbnb.com

Yes, the Avalon is on Duval Street but at the far southwest end, the opposite end of Duval's bar district. Here you'll find mostly galleries and coffee shops. The Key West Butterfly & Nature Conservatory is across the street. The southernmost point buoy is two blocks around the corner. This two-story house is thought to have been built sometime in the mid-1880s. Owner Emilio Aymerich operated a school downstairs, and the upstairs was likely a residential apartment. Key West's Cuban Club met there as well before moving up the street a few years later. The Cuban Club would continue its affiliation with the building, though. Dr. Nilo Pintado opened a hospital in the house in 1917 and offered free medical services to Cuban Club members.

A couple of the Avalon's ten rooms face Duval Street, but most overlook the garden and pool behind the house. There's also a one-bedroom cottage that opens on to the pool as well.

Blue Parrot Inn
916 Elizabeth Street
Key West 33040
(305) 296-0033
(800) 231-2473
www.blueparrotinn.com

This charming 1884 house is one of several built by Walter C. Maloney for one of his seven children. Maloney was the mayor of Key West,

BLUE PARROT INN

the editor of the *Key West Dispatch,* and also the author of Key West's first history, *A Sketch of the History of Key West, Florida,* published in 1876. The Blue Parrot has been a bed-and-breakfast since 1985. Owners Diane Hadley and Landon Bradbury also own Authors of Key West Guesthouse.

Casa Marina Resort
1500 Reynolds Street
Key West 33040
(888) 303-5717
www.casamarinaresort.com

The Casa Marina was to be railroad magnate Henry Flagler's last hotel, but he never got to see the groundbreaking. Construction began in 1918 and was completed in 1921, eight years after Flagler's death. (See A Tale of Two Henrys following my Introduction.) It is the oldest operating hotel in Key West. Like the rest of Key West (and Florida), the Case Marina struggled throughout the 1930s, but it was during this decade that famous poets Robert Frost and Wallace Stevens stayed there. During World War II, the hotel closed and became a military hospital and officers' quarters.

Marriot purchased and thoroughly restored the three-story hotel in 1978. In 1999 the Wyndham Hotel chain bought it and then sold it to LXR Resorts. In 2009 it was acquired by Waldorf Astoria Hotels.

CASA MARINA RESORT

Each successive owner has added its own renovations, and Waldorf Astoria's $43-million renovation included redesigning the lobby and rebuilding the pool area. The Casa Marina is an elegant hotel with two pools, its own private beach, and 311 luxurious rooms in a variety of sizes, including a 900-square-foot, two-story suite with two bedrooms and two baths.

Conch House Heritage Inn
625 Truman Avenue
Key West 33040
(305) 293-0020
(800) 207-5806
www.conchhouse.com

Key West wholesale grocery business owner Carlos Recio purchased this two-story 1889 home in 1895. Recio was a friend of Cuban revolutionary José Martí, and he helped him raise funds and smuggle

CONCH HOUSE HERITAGE INN

supplies to the revolutionaries on merchant ships. The word Heritage in the inn's name is significant because the Conch House has remained in Recio's family for generations. Today it's owned and operated by his great-granddaughter Francine Holland and great-great-grandson Sam Holland. The house underwent a thorough restoration in 1993 and is listed on the National Register of Historic Places. There are ten rooms in the main house and in adjacent cottages.

Curry Mansion
511 Caroline Street
Key West 33040
(305) 294-5349
(800) 253-3466
www.currymansion.com

The Curry name is synonymous with Key West's golden era, a time when adventurers populated the island. Wrecking–the salvaging of cargo from ships that foundered on the reefs–had turned Key West into one of the richest cities per capita in the United States by the mid-1800s. Some enterprising folks did well in businesses that provisioned the wrecking industry. One such entrepreneur was William Curry, most certainly Key West's, and quite possibly Florida's, first millionaire.

Curry's ancestors were Scottish Loyalists who abandoned their Carolina plantation during the Revolutionary War and fled to Green Turtle Cay in the Bahamas. In 1837 sixteen-year-old William left the family home for the promise of fortunes to be made in Key West. By 1845 he was a partner in a ship supply and outfitting business. Curry's father-in-law, wrecking Captain John Lowe, soon joined the business and expanded it into an operation with a fleet of wrecking schooners. By the 1850s, William Curry was the wealthiest man in the Keys and had broadened his interests to include banking, tugboats, and an icehouse. In 1861 he bought out his partners and renamed the business Curry and Sons.

William Curry died in 1896, and his son Milton inherited the family homestead on Caroline Street, which had been built in 1855. Milton's wife, Elaine, the daughter of a local banker, apparently felt that the Curry home was too modest. In 1905 she ordered it remodeled. By the time she was through with it, nothing remained of the original home except the kitchen.

Elaine Curry certainly had good taste. The grand, three-story mansion borrows its Colonial Revival style from a Newport, Rhode Island, "cottage" that Milton and Elaine saw while on their honeymoon. Shipbuilding carpenters did most of the work on Key West homes back then, and it was not unusual for them to reuse salvaged pieces from wrecked ships, like brass railings and portholes, in their construction. Their meticulous craftsmanship shows in the Curry Mansion, with its intricate, exterior scrollwork trimmed in gold and bird's-eye maple paneling on the interior walls. A rooftop cupola, or poop deck, accessible by ladder from the third floor offers a 360-degree view of the island and surrounding ocean. Milton probably kept watch on the family fleet from there.

As grand as it was when the Currys lived there, the house had become a run-down rooming house by the time Edith and Al Amsterdam bought it in 1975. It was the Amsterdams' private home until 1988, when they opened the Curry Mansion as both a bed-and-breakfast and a museum. They furnished the mansion with antiques collected from their families or acquired from around Key West. Among these is an 1853 Chickering piano once owned by author Henry James.

There are twenty-two rooms and suites in the original mansion, eight more in the James House across the street (added in 1994), plus an additional twenty-eight in the adjacent Guest Wing. I stayed in the Owner's Suite on the second floor of the mansion. Edith and Al lived in it for many years before moving across the hall. It has a four-poster canopy bed that backs up to a bay window in the master bedroom, a separate sitting room, and French doors that open onto a huge veranda. Al Amsterdam passed away in 2001, and Edith continues to run the Curry Mansion.

Duval House
815 Duval Street
Key West 33040
(305) 292-9491
www.duvalhousekeywest.com

Duval House, midway down Duval Street, has thirty rooms and suites in seven Victorian Conch houses surrounding a garden courtyard and pool.

Heron House
512 Simonton Street
Key West 33040
(305) 294-9227
(800) 294-1644

Heron House Court
412 Francis Street
Key West 33040
(800) 932-9119
www.heronhouse.com

Heron House has two locations. The original Simonton Street property consists of four circa-1850s buildings. There are twenty-three

HERON HOUSE

rooms and suites set in an exquisite tropical garden filled with orchids, all surrounding a pool and upper-level sundeck. The tropical theme extends seamlessly into the rooms, which are decorated with rattan, bright fabrics, and watercolor paintings. The newer Heron House Court is five blocks down the road. This was originally a turn-of-the-century quarters for workers constructing Henry Flagler's railroad, and it has a bit more of a boutique hotel feel. Heron House Court has fourteen rooms, two of which are suites.

Historic Key West Inns
www.historickeywestinns.com

Historic Key West Inns is a collection of six previously independent Key West inns and bed-and-breakfasts. Julia Fondriest founded the company in 1997 when she purchased the Merlin Guesthouse. Next she bought the Cactus Terrace Motor Court/Maloney House property and turned it into the Key Lime Inn. Over the years she has steadily added properties, the most recent the Cypress House. The next six listings are all Historic Key West Inns properties.

Albury Court
1030 Eaton Street
Key West 33040
(305) 294-9870
(877) 299-9870
www.historickeywestinns.com

This boutique hotel has thirty-eight rooms in five buildings, situated in a residential part of Key West's Old Town. There's also a pool with a waterfall.

Chelsea House
709 Truman Avenue
Key West 33040
(305) 296-2211
(800) 845-8859
www.historickeywestinns.com

Chelsea House consists of two grand Victorian mansions. The original Chelsea House was built in 1921 by George L. Lowe, a well-respected banker whose family was in the mercantile and lumber business. Then there is the Delgato House next door, which has a much more colorful history. Before the two were combined, the Delgato House was the Red Rooster Inn. The house was built in the 1870s and was home to the Delgato family, who were in the cigar manufacturing business. One day Mr. Delgato disappeared, never to be seen again. Most assumed he had returned to Cuba, but decades later, on her deathbed, Mrs. Delgato confessed to murdering him and burying his body underneath the front porch. Curiously, I couldn't find any more information on this incident. Did anyone ever dig up the front porch to look? What I did find was some later history. This was a Coast Guard living quarters for a while. Then, in the 1950s and 1960s, it had a dubious reputation as a brothel and a wild party house.

Today it seems things are much calmer. Between the two houses there are thirty-three attractively renovated rooms, including two upstairs suites with private porches, vaulted ceilings, and kitchenettes. There's also a large, heated pool and sundeck area. So who is Chelsea? Apparently she was a cat that lived at the Lowe house in the 1970s.

CHELSEA HOUSE

Cypress House
601 Caroline Street
Key West, Florida 33040
(305) 294-6969
(800) 525-2488
www.historickeywestinns.com

John T. Sawyer built this Bahamian-style mansion in 1887 after the previous structure burned during Key West's 1886 fire. In the Key West Directory for 1888, Sawyer, an apparent jack-of-all-trades, is listed as a "Dealer in Groceries and Confectionary, and Builder and Contractor." He built the home for Richard M. Kemp, a furniture dealer who was more famously the self-taught naturalist who identified and named the Kemp's Ridley sea turtle. The house is easy to spot because its exterior has been left unpainted, as were many of the homes in Key West prior to the turn of the century. The house is built from both pine and cypress and has tall, exterior louvered shutters on the windows and the doors, another Bahamian feature. The twenty-two-room Cypress House is rich with old Key West character but is outfitted with plenty of modern accouterments, including a forty-foot-long heated lap pool. Cypress House is Historic Key West Inns' newest acquisition, purchased in 2012.

CYPRESS HOUSE

Key Lime Inn
725 Truman Avenue
Key West 33040
(305) 294-5229
(800) 549-4430
www.historickeywestinns.com

Key Lime Inn occupies a veritable compound that was once the prominent Maloney family's estate (see the Blue Parrot Inn entry). In 1939 Joseph "Suicide" Zorsky, a circus entertainer, bought the property from the Maloneys. Zorsky added twelve cottages and opened the Cactus Terrace Motor Court. Today there are thirty-seven rooms in the assortment of cottages and in the main 1854 Maloney House. The entire property underwent a complete transformation in 1999.

Lighthouse Court
902 Whitehead Street
Key West 33040
(305) 294-9588
(877) 294-9588
www.historickeywestinns.com

Lighthouse Court has forty rooms and suites in ten Conch cottages built between 1890 and 1920. They sit right next door to Key West's 1848 Lighthouse and Museum and across the street from the historic Ernest Hemingway House. Lighthouse Court also has the poolside Mojito Bar & Café.

LIGHTHOUSE COURT

Merlin Guesthouse
811 Simonton Street
Key West 33040
(305) 296-3336
(800) 642-4753
www.historickeywestinns.com

The Merlin Guesthouse was Julia Fondriest's first Historic Key West Inns acquisition. The main inn was a Navy personnel boardinghouse built in 1930. It has ten rooms, and there are ten more rooms in a selection of cottages around the main inn. The name refers to Merlin Albury, who was Key Largo's postmaster from 1910 until the 1920s before arriving in Key West. The Albury families were true Conchs who had moved to the Upper Keys from the Bahamas.

La Concha Crowne Plaza Hotel
430 Duval Street
Key West 33040
(305) 296-2991
www.laconchakeywest.com

At seven stories, the La Concha Hotel, a Key West icon built in 1926, is the tallest building on the island. The first six floors are hotel rooms, and the seventh is a rooftop bar that affords Key West's best view across the city.

Developer Carl Aubuchon most often gets credit for building the La Concha, but I found more complete information in an October 10, 1924, *Key West Citizen* newspaper article archived at the University of Florida Library. The company that built the La Concha was the Florida Keys Realty Company. Carl Aubuchon was listed as vice president. Curiously I could find no more information about Aubuchon anywhere else, but I did find plenty of information about the president of the company, attorney Jefferson B. Browne. Browne was a key player in Key West from the 1880s through the 1930s: He was a city attorney, postmaster, Florida senator, head of the Key West Customs Office, chairman of the Florida Railroad Commission, Florida Supreme Court chief justice, and Miami and Key West circuit court judge. He also wrote a history volume entitled *Key West, The Old and the New* in 1912. He died in 1937. It seems apparent that Browne handled the red tape and Aubuchon handled the actual contracting. Atlanta architectural firm G. Lloyd Preacher and Company did the design. State Bank and Trust offices were the anchor and occupied the first floor. Florida Keys Realty Company's press release claimed the building cost $768,000 to build.

Fires were very much a concern in Key West. An 1886 fire, thought to have been set by Spanish forces in opposition to the Cuban Revolution, had burned a significant portion of downtown Key West and particularly its cigar factories. So the new La Concha—built with a steel frame, marble floors, and terra cotta exterior—was heavily advertised as fireproof. It opened with much fanfare in January 1926. Broadway star Martha Lane was the headliner. But four years later, following the 1929 stock market crash, not just the La Concha but all of Key West would be in a precipitous economic decline. The hotel was sold in 1930 and renamed the Key West Colonial Hotel, but everybody still called it the La Concha.

There are some literary and historical footnotes associated with the hotel: In Ernest Hemingway's 1937 *To Have and Have Not,* character Harry Morgan notes that the La Concha is his sight guide for returning to Key West from Cuba. Tennessee Williams lived in a top-floor suite at the La Concha for a year and finished writing *A Streetcar Named Desire* there in 1947.

Although the La Concha managed to remain open for decades, it continued to decay. By the 1970s, only a downstairs diner and the rooftop bar remained open. The La Concha would not recover until

LA CONCHA CROWNE PLAZA HOTEL

Holiday Inn bought the dilapidated property and embarked on a multimillion-dollar restoration in 1986. Subsequently, Crowne Plaza Hotels (now a part of Intercontinental Hotels Group) purchased Holiday Inn. In 2012 the hotel was renovated once again. This time the rooms were updated, including the sixth-floor two-bedroom suite where Tennessee Williams lived. In addition to The Top, the hotel's rooftop bar, the La Concha also features Jack's Seafood Restaurant and the island's only Starbucks coffee shop.

Like so many old historic hotels, the La Concha has some ghost stories. One of the most often told concerns a man who was helping clean up The Top bar on New Year's Eve in 1982. He was pulling a cart of dirty plates and backed through a freight elevator's open doors, unaware that the elevator had not arrived yet on that floor. Some people claim that his ghost appears on the fifth floor, even though he fell from the sixth floor, and some report hearing his scream as he falls down the elevator shaft.

La Mer and Dewey House Bed & Breakfast
504–506 South Street
Key West 33040
(305) 296-6577
(800) 354-4455
www.southernmostresorts.com

Southernmost Hotel Collection operates three properties at Duval Street's much quieter southwest end, the opposite end from Duval's party district. Here you'll find more galleries and coffee shops than bars. The Southernmost collection includes La Mer and Dewey House and Southernmost on the Beach, both on the waterfront, and Southernmost Hotel across the street. I much prefer this end of Duval and have stayed there numerous times. I try to avoid naming my personal favorites in my guidebooks, but, oh well, I'll make an exception. La Mer and Dewey House, two historic houses that have been combined into one bed-and-breakfast, is my favorite place to stay in Key West. The Dewey House is named for philosopher, psychologist, and Columbia University professor John Dewey, who purchased the circa-1906 house with wife Roberta in 1944, when Dewey was eighty-five years old. Despite his age, Dewey continued to write and publish while in Key West. He died in New York in 1952. The circa-1910 La Mer House belonged to architect D.B. Walker, who built it as his family home. The two houses share an open-air lobby and breakfast area that opens onto Southernmost's own beach. There are nineteen rooms and suites with French doors that open onto private porches and balconies. Of course, guests have full access to Southernmost's fitness center, three pools, two bars, and Beachfront Café.

LA MER AND DEWEY HOUSE BED & BREAKFAST

L'Habitation Guest House
408 Eaton Street
Key West 33040
(305) 293-9203
(800) 697-1766
www.lhabitation.com

This circa-1874 house, a block off Duval on Eaton Street, was the Tides Guest House in the 1950s. Today it has eleven rooms, including one large two-bedroom suite. While its owners do serve coffee, tea, and pastries in the morning, they don't claim to run a bed-and-breakfast.

Marquesa Hotel
600 Fleming Street
Key West 33040
(305) 292-1919
www.marquesa.com

The Marquesa Hotel, at the corner of Simonton and Fleming Streets, was originally the home of Key West butcher James Haskins. He built it in 1884 and somehow dodged the 1886 fire that burned down houses only a block away. In 1889 he leased out a portion of the bottom floor to a gentleman's clothing store. In 1893 it became Dr. Burgos' pharmacy. Later it was an office for the Key West Gas Company. But from 1939 to 1949, it housed a longtime Key West landmark, Fausto's Grocery Store. Faustino Castillo arrived in Key West from Cuba in 1910 to work in the cigar-making business. Sixteen years later, he had saved enough money to open a tiny grocery store in a house on Virginia Street, a block from the main drag, Truman Avenue. By 1939 the store had outgrown the house, and Faustino moved it to the location that is now the Marquesa Hotel. That first-floor section that was Fausto's is now Marquesa's lobby and its restaurant, Café Marquesa. Fausto's Grocery is still in business with two stores: one a block away from the Marquesa on Fleming, the other on White Street.

The last Haskins family member to own the property left it to an order of Catholic nuns in the 1970s. It had become a rundown boarding house when Erik deBoer and Richard Manley purchased it in 1987. They spent $1.5 million restoring the building and adding a wing. Then in 1993, they bought the two adjacent buildings and spent another $2.2 million to renovate and integrate them into the existing property.

With twenty-seven rooms and suites, the Marquesa is by all accounts one of Key West's finest boutique hotels, and it is certainly one my favorites. I stayed in a corner room in the main building at the top of the stairs. Afternoon light filtered through the gumbo-limbo tree that grows next to the side window, giving the sky-blue room an outdoors-like glow. Although it's a small room, it has one big feature: its own twenty-foot-long balcony, with a comfy wicker rocker

MARQUESA HOTEL

and a love seat with overstuffed cushions. The room and the balcony overlook the neighborhood on tree-shaded Fleming Street. Most of Key West watched the sunset from Mallory Square, but I watched it from that cozy rocking chair. The largest suites open onto a palm-shaded, tropical garden courtyard with two swimming pools and a waterfall.

The most difficult decision a visitor to Key West has to make is where to have dinner. Choose the Café Marquesa and you will never be disappointed. The menu changes daily, but to give you an idea of the fare, on my last visit I had chilled potato-and-leek vichyssoise with flying fish roe and sesame-crusted yellowtail snapper in mango sauce. I'm getting hungry just writing about it.

Mermaid & the Alligator
729 Truman Avenue
Key West 33040
(305) 294-1894
(800) 773-1894
www.kwmermaid.com

Key West city attorney Norvin Maloney built this three-story Queen Anne Victorian in 1904. Norvin's grandfather, Walter C. Maloney (see the Blue Parrot Inn entry), owned most of this block, as well as other property nearby where various Maloney family members built homes. The Mermaid & the Alligator is surrounded by a lush tropical garden. The name comes from the Wilbur Thomas sculpture in the garden. There are six rooms and suites in the main house, plus three more in the Conch Cottage. The Treetop Suite, tucked beneath the roof gable on the third floor, has vaulted ceilings and a splendid view across Old Town Key West. Owners Dean Carlson and Paul Hayes are avid dog lovers, and if you visit you will likely be greeted by one of their friendly flat-coated retrievers.

MERMAID & THE ALLIGATOR

Paradise Inn
819 Simonton Street
Key West 33040
(305) 293-8007
(800) 888-9648
www.theparadiseinn.com

Paradise Inn blends the old with the new. Historic cottages and two new Bahamian-style houses surround a meticulously landscaped garden courtyard with gumbo-limbo trees, a variety of exotic plants and flowers, a koi pond, a hot tub, and a pool.

Santa Maria Suites
1401 Simonton Street
Key West 33040
(305) 296-5678
(866) 726-8259
www.santamariasuites.com

What was originally a classic 1950s' Florida motel has been rebuilt into a glossy tropical modern–style boutique hotel (think the Jetsons meet Brickell Avenue). Santa Maria Suites has thirty-five one- and two-bedroom (and two-bath) suites with full state-of-the-art kitchens that include Jenn-Air stoves, Sub-Zero refrigerators, and wine chillers. Sleek, contemporary furnishings and lots of stone tile, marble, stainless steel, and glass carry the modern theme inside. The suites surround and overlook two pools and a garden courtyard where happy hour is served daily. I stayed at the Santa Maria in 2007 just a few months after it opened and was entranced the minute I walked through the door. Santa Maria is also located at my favorite end of the island, two blocks from the southernmost point. Its on-site restaurant, Ambrosia, specializes in sushi, tempura, and other Japanese dishes.

SANTA MARIA SUITES

Tropical Inn
812 Duval Street
Key West 33040
(305) 294-9977
(888) 611-6510
www.tropicalinn.com

Tropical Inn's six rooms in the main house and five cottage rooms are all decorated in bright, tropical colors. Although the inn fronts busy Duval Street, its lush garden and pool courtyard are an oasis nicely isolated from Duval Street activity. The upstairs Key Lime Loft and Banyan Tree Suite have private balconies overlooking the garden and pool. The property has been an inn since 1984. Current owners Jane Lowe and Allen Lewis of Savannah purchased the Tropical Inn in 1999.

Weatherstation Inn
57 Front Street
Key West 33040
(305) 294-7277
(800) 815-2707
www.weatherstationinn.com

This stately inn occupies what was once a United States Weather Bureau Station. The National Weather Service was first established in 1870 as a division of the United States Army, with twenty-four stations around the country. Key West's observation station was one of those initial twenty-four and certainly one of the most vital. It was the station's job to telegraph rainfall measurements and other meteorological data on a daily basis to Washington, D.C. The station had several temporary locations for its first thirty years before building a permanent station on the corner of Front and Eaton Streets. But in 1910, a hurricane flooded the building and forced a move to the Island City Bank Building on Duval Street for two years while the Front Street station was rebuilt. It reopened on Front Street in January 1913, and the building served as the Weather Bureau Station there until 1957, when the United States Navy began using it as servicemen's quarters until the Navy Base Annex closed in 1974. Tim and Kelly Koenig bought the building in 1992 as their private home and in 1995 decided to turn it into a bed-and-breakfast. Subsequently, Ocean Properties purchased it and opened the Weatherstation Inn in 1997. Weatherstation Inn has eight rooms and a heated swimming pool and serves a continental breakfast.

INDEX

Here are some other books from Pineapple Press on related topics. For a complete catalog, write to Pineapple Press, P.O. Box 3889, Sarasota, Florida 34230-3889, or call (800) 746-3275. Or visit our website at www.pineapplepress.com.

Visiting Small-Town Florida, Third Edition, by Bruce Hunt. From Carrabelle to Bokeelia, Two Egg to Fernandina, these out-of-the-way but fascinating destinations are well worth a side trip or weekend excursion. A guide to 75 of Florida's most interesting small towns.

Historic Homes of Florida, Second Edition, by Laura Stewart and Susanne Hupp. Houses tell the human side of history. In this survey of restored residences, their stories are intertwined with those of their owners in a domestic history of Florida. Most of these houses are museums now; others are restaurants or bed-and-breakfasts. This new edition is updated and illustrated with color photographs.

Florida's Museums and Cultural Attractions, Second Edition, by Doris Bardon and Murray D. Laurie. This newly updated guide has a destination to suit every interest. You'll find more than 350 museums and attractions to choose from.

Houses of St. Augustine by David Nolan. Photographs by Ken Barrett Jr.; watercolors by Jean Ellen Fitzpatrick. A comprehensive and fully illustrated book of the architecture of the Spanish, British, and American periods in the Ancient City. Full color.

Flagler's St. Augustine Hotels by Thomas Graham. Describes Henry Flagler's three lavish hotels in St. Augustine. The Ponce de Leon, Flagler's preeminent hotel, now houses Flagler College. The Alcazar now holds City Hall and the Lightner Museum. The Casa Monica (previously called the Cordova) has been restored as a hotel. Full-color photographs.

St. Augustine and St. Johns County: A Historical Guide by William R. Adams. A guide to the places and buildings where history can be found in America's oldest permanent settlement. Features color photographs throughout.

Historical Traveler's Guide to Florida, Second Edition, by Eliot Kleinberg. From Fort Pickens in the Panhandle to Fort Jefferson in the ocean 40 miles beyond Key West, historical travelers will find many adventures waiting for them in Florida. Eliot Kleinberg—whose vocation, avocation, and obsession is Florida history—has poked around the state looking for the most fascinating historic places to visit. In this second edition, he presents 74 of his favorites—17 of them are new to this edition, and the rest have been completely updated.

Time Traveler's Guide to Florida by Jack Powell. A unique guidebook that describes 70 places and reenactments in Florida where you can experience the past—and a few where you can time-travel into the future.

Best Backroads of Florida by Douglas Waitley. Each volume in this series offers several well-planned day trips through some of Florida's least-known towns and well-traveled byways. You will glimpse a gentler Florida and learn a lot about its history. Volume 1: *The Heartland* (south of Jacksonville to north of Tampa); Volume 2: *Coasts, Glades, and Groves* (south Florida); Volume 3: *Beaches and Hills* (north and northwest Florida).

Florida History from the Highways by Douglas Waitley. Journey along Florida's highways—I-75, US 41, I-95, US 27, US 98, and the Turnpike—learning all the roadside history along the way. Begins with a brief history of Florida.

Exploring Wild South Florida, Fourth Edition, by Susan Jewell. From West Palm Beach to Fort Myers and south through the Everglades and Florida Keys lie the world-renowned wetlands and coral reefs that have long enticed people seeking unique, year-round outdoor experiences. This updated edition covers federal, state, county, municipal, and private lands in Broward, Collier, Hendry, Lee, Miami-Dade, Monroe, and Palm Beach Counties, including more than 20 new locations. Hikers, paddlers, bicyclists, wildlife watchers, and campers will find information on how to access the natural areas, when to go, and how to ensure your visit is enjoyable and safe.

CPSIA information can be obtained at www.ICGtesting.com
Printed in the USA
BVOW08s1133030913

329889BV00007B/17/P